THE QUANT
INVESTOR'S
ALMANAC
2011

THE QUANT INVESTOR'S ALMANAC 2011

A ROADMAP TO INVESTING

IRENE ALDRIDGE

STEVEN KRAWCIW

WILEY

John Wiley & Sons, Inc.

Published by John Wiley & Sons, Inc., Hoboken, New Jersey.

Published simultaneously in Canada.

For general information on our other products and services or for technical support,
please contact our Customer Care Department within the United States at
(800) 762-2974, outside the United States at (317) 572-3993 or fax (317) 572-4002.

Wiley also publishes its books in a variety of electronic formats. Some content that
appears in print may not be available in electronic books. For more information about
Wiley products, visit our web site at www.wiley.com.

ISBN 978-0-470-63561-2 (paper); 978-0-470-90964-5 (ebk); 978-0-470-90961-4 (ebk)

Printed in the United States of America

10 9 8 7 6 5 4 3 2 1

CONTENTS

Preface   vii

Introduction to Quantitative Investing   1

January
New Ideas In Quant Investing
Strategies: Stocks   15

February
Cutting-Edge Quant Investing Strategies:
Foreign Exchange, Mutual Funds, and ETFs   27

March
National Output and Income   39

April
Sectoral Production, Orders, and
Inventories   53

May
Consumer Spending and Confidence   67

June
Housing and Construction   79

July
Foreign Trade and International
Capital Flow   91

August

Employment   103

September

Prices, Wages, and Productivity   115

October

Monetary and Financial Data   129

November

Federal Reserve Policy and Federal
Government Finances   141

December

Innovative Trading Ideas   153

Glossary   165

References   179

About the Authors   183

Index   185

PREFACE

For years, quantitative investing was regarded as the domain of a select few institutional traders that employed teams of highly educated mathematicians and physicists. Yet, many principles behind quantitative investing are surprisingly easy to understand and boil down to common sense.

This Almanac is one of the first books to offer investors of all stripes the latest quantitative investing strategies digested down to their essentials.

Who should read this Almanac:

- Institutional traders/fund managers
- Brokers and private bankers
- HNW traders managing their own accounts
- Individual investors

Why you should read this Almanac:

- To learn how to trade using quantitative techniques.
- To know when announcements are scheduled to hit the news.
- To understand how these announcements have moved the markets in the past.

The quantitative investing ideas presented in this Almanac appeal to both institutional and individual investors. Unlike academic periodicals where many quantitative investment strategies are first published, this Almanac avoids scientific jargon and focuses on the central thesis of selected research. Ample suggestions for further reading are supplied throughout the text for readers interested in additional information and strategy details.

The field of quantitative investing is extremely broad and includes investments in complicated financial structures. To keep matters accessible to every investor, the Almanac focuses on just several categories of quantitative strategies. These are:

- Macroeconomic event investing across various asset categories
- Mutual funds
- Stocks (equity)
- Bonds (fixed income)
- Foreign exchange
- Exchange traded funds (ETFs)
- Futures
- Options

At the core of the Almanac are the latest quantitative investing strategies condensed into short articles designed to explain to the reader the key idea behind each investment strategy. The Almanac purposefully excludes complicated details when discussing quantitative investing strategies. No special prerequisites are required to follow the discussions. No mathematical prowess, computer knowledge, or economic education is necessary.

The Almanac is written for investors who want to learn about quantitative investing strategies. Professional quantitative traders and portfolio managers should also find the book useful as it provides a brief digest of the latest ideas developed in the field of quantitative finance. Should the reader be interested in learning more about a particular topic from the Almanac, thorough references to original academic and practitioner research are provided to point the reader in the direction of further details.

As our world becomes increasingly global, so do quantitative investment strategies. With the rise of the Internet, many brokerages offer investors

from one country securities from another region. While many stock (equity), bond (fixed income) and options strategies apply in most financial
markets, strategies driven by local political, fiscal, and regulatory activity
tend to have the highest impact in their own jurisdiction. The Almanac includes dates, times, and impact analyses of selected macroeconomic events
scheduled to take place in the United States, Canada, United Kingdom,
European Union, and selected other countries, to enable investors to deploy
quantitative strategies in various markets around the world.

Many macroeconomic events recur weekly, monthly, or annually. Like
sailors using the lunar cycles to determine the ebbs and flows in chart-
ing their course, many quantitative investors keep in mind the economic
indicators and their historical impact in determining their investment
decisions.

The book is structured as follows: The Introduction presents an overview of the key aspects of quantitative investing. The 12 subsequent sections
(each corresponding to a month of the year) outline the latest quantitative
investment strategies. Many strategies are related to the release of particular
economic figures. The dates and times of these figures are compiled in the
calendar pages of the Almanac. While the quantitative investing strategies
are grouped into distinct months, according to their subject, the grouping
generally has little connection with the actual month of the calendar where
the investment strategy appears in the Almanac—the reader is encouraged
to read through the entire Almanac at once. A glossary at the end of the
book describes key quant investing terminology and can be used as a refer-
ence for various quant topics.

Icons are used throughout the book to show the topic of a particular
event listing. For example, the same icon will be used throughout the book
to identify events related to employment or the release of employment data.
The icons used are as follows:

Consumer Spending	🛒
Employment	💼
U.S. Federal Reserve Actions	💵

Foreign Trade	
Housing	
Monetary Data	
National Output	
Prices	
Production	

This Almanac is by no means designed to be comprehensive. Readers seeking the most exceptional coverage of trading strategies are encouraged to browse through the top academic literature in finance. The three sources most often referenced herein are the *Journal of Finance*, the *Journal of Financial Economics*, and the *Review of Financial Studies*. All three often require an advanced academic background in finance, economics, and statistics (econometrics), although readers may acquire the necessary knowledge by persistently perusing the journals.

While the Almanac shares with its readers specific investment prescriptions, the strategies discussed herein by no means constitute investment advice. The authors and their employers disclaim all responsibility for the application of the discussed trading strategies. Readers are encouraged to consult their investment advisors when allocating capital in their own accounts. As always, the readers should consider their individual risk tolerances, investment objectives, and other relevant characteristics of their portfolios. Readers are encouraged to peruse the full liabillity/disclaimer language appearing on the copyright page of the Almanac.

INTRODUCTION TO QUANTITATIVE INVESTING

T he *Quant Investor's Almanac 2011* brings the principles of quantitative investing from Wall Street to every Main Street investor.

Quantitative investing has recently garnered attention as a significant advance as practitioners have time and again outperformed investing benchmarks, delivering superior returns to their employers and clients.

This Introduction explores the basics of quantitative investing, and key considerations in managing one's portfolio within a quantitative framework.

WHAT IS QUANTITATIVE INVESTING?

Q uantitative investing refers to investment strategies verified using quantitative techniques that incorporate statistical analysis, economic theory, and other scientific tools and mathematical experiments. This investing methodology comprises the identification of persistent factors and phenomena driving changes in asset prices. Rather than making investment decisions exclusively based on subjective information, this methodology introduces statistical techniques to investment management. Once the factors are identified for analysis, a quantitative investor uses factor values to decide whether a particular security is overpriced or underpriced. He then buys securities deemed underpriced, sells securities deemed overpriced, or waits for other securities to clear.

Quantitative investing can be "long-only" and "long-short." In finance, being "long" in a particular security means buying this security, and selling securities only to close out a position. Long-only investors buy securities

1

with the expectation that prices will appreciate. Mutual funds practice long-only investing.

Long-short quantitative investing allows for "shorting" securities in addition to going long in them. To go "short" in a security means to sell the security without buying it first. The shorting investor merely borrows the security from his broker or another investor, sells it in the open market, and then repurchases the security and returns it to its original holder at a later date. In shorting, the investor anticipates the prices of the shorted securities to drop. Hedge funds practice long-short investing.

Whether an investor is long-only or long-short does not say anything about the investor's position-holding duration. Both long-only and long-short investors can reallocate positions frequently, or not so often. Both long-only and long-short investors who reallocate their positions often are said to practice "dynamic trading." Long-only investors who keep their positions for weeks, months, or even years at a time practice "buy-and-hold" strategies.

Dynamic investors care mostly about high-frequency returns of trading in financial securities. These returns are based on relatively small changes in temporarily distorted prices that may occur in the markets for a variety of reasons. On the other hand, buy-and-hold investors focus on the price levels. While many quantitative investing strategies apply to both types of investors, some strategies are best suited for dynamic investors only, and some are best used by buy-and-hold investors.

How Does It Work?

One of the advantages of quantitative investment strategies is that they are well suited to the development of trading signals.

In a nutshell, a trading process based on a quantitative investment strategy works in these three stages:

1. First, the quantitative strategy is used to determine the price of a given security (stock, currency, commodity, option, etc.). The investor seeks to answer the following question: Is the given security overpriced or underpriced according to the particular quantitative investment strategy?

2. If the security is deemed overpriced (underpriced) according to the quantitative model, sell (buy) the security.

3. Close the position by buying (selling) back the security when one of the following conditions is met.

   - The security price reaches the target price prescribed by the quantitative investment model.

   - The security realizes a gain deemed sufficient, also known as "stop-gain."

   - The security price moves adversely and realizes a maximum loss deemed tolerable. The position is closed out to limit further losses. This is a common "stop-loss" risk-management tactic. The stop-loss level is determined before the position is opened. The acceptable stop-loss may depend on the volatility of the security, initial price levels, and past price history.

These orders are typically transmitted electronically, yet many quant strategies with long holding periods can still be executed over the phone.

How Does It Differ from Traditional Investing?

Quantitative models bring discipline and clarity to investing. Unlike traditional (or discretionary) investing, where the investor often relies on his "intuition" to make investment decisions, quantitative investing offers a precise scientific rationale for each investment decision. In addition, quantitative models provide explicitly measurable performance expectations for each investment strategy, making it easier to allocate capital and manage one's investments.

Overview of Trading Strategies

The development of quantitative strategies involves more mathematical modeling and less intuition than is typical of more traditional approaches. Yet, quant strategies are not in conflict with value investing; rather, these strategies precisely measure distortions in value that complement longer term trends at the core of value investing.

Quantitative investment strategies are known as such for three main reasons.

1. Inputs into the investment decisions are quantified, i.e., expressed in numerical format.
2. Strategies are tested on historical data to ensure that the chosen inputs indeed perform well.
3. Strategies are based on firm mathematical relationships.

Regardless of how many inputs are fed into a strategy, and how complex are the mathematical relationships underpinning the strategies, at the end of the day most quantitative strategies boil down to a very simple framework: Buy a share of stock X when its price falls below $Y, and sell the same share of stock X when its price rises above $Z. The most difficult and important part in developing quantitative strategies is the determining the levels $Y and $Z.

Quant investment strategies can encompass all traditional investing styles with discretion supplemented by mathematical relationships. As such, quant strategies can be both technical and fundamental. Technical quant strategies rely on mathematical recognition of patterns and involve the disciplined application of advanced statistics, known as econometrics. Fundamental quant strategies use core economic relationships between security prices and economic variables to arrive at the investable price levels $Y and $Z.

Besides technical and fundamental strategies, quant investment strategies include an array of methods based entirely on statistical relationships among two or more securities. Such strategies are often referred to as "statistical arbitrage."

How Are They Discovered?

When searching for quantitative investment strategies, most investment managers follow one of these approaches:

- Top-down
- Bottom-up

In the top-down approach, an investor observes a market phenomenon that he believes may be tradable, and then uses quantitative methodology to prove his hunch. The market phenomenon in question may be a rise in stock prices following a specific news announcement, a jump in the foreign exchange rate after a rise in a price of a futures contract, and a variety of other occurrences that the investor believes to be persistent, that is, occurring over and over again.

At this stage in the quant investor's conjecture, the observation of a reccurrence is known as a "hypothesis." Once the hypothesis is identified, the investor tests it on historical data by identifying similar market conditions and estimating contemporaneous response in prices. If the price response repeats itself in a statistically significant manner, the hypothesis is considered valid, and the strategy is given a green light.

In the bottom-up approach, the quant investor seeks to identify a tradable phenomenon by applying statistical tests to large quantities of data in the hope of discerning a persistent relationship. The data may include prices of securities, economic indicators, as well as other variables. The bottom-up approach is sometimes referred to as "data-mining."

This approach carries the risk of finding spurious relationships that are accidents in the data and may not form the basis of a persistent trading strategy. It is the test of effective due diligence to find patterns that are actually tradable.

It is also important to note that top-down and bottom-up patterns are not permanent. Tradeable distortions may exist for a reason that can in itself be time-limited, capping the useful life of a quantitative strategy.

Yet, both top-down and bottom-up approaches can produce long-term profitable investment strategies, particularly if the discovery is persistent and makes sense from an economic point of view. For example, an observation that the price of a foreign exchange rate consistently falls in response to increases in inflation can be validated from an economic point of view, and it is likely to persist going forward. On the other hand, a constant range in prices of two seemingly unrelated stocks may be just a coincidental or "spurious" relationship, and lacking any other theoretical or experimental support.

WHICH PHENOMENA HAVE THE MOST IMPACT AND WHEN?

As a general rule, the impact of the observed phenomenon depends on the origin of the phenomenon. Broad market announcements tend to impact most securities, albeit to different degrees. Announcements concerning a particular industry are likely to affect securities issued within that industry as well as those issued by their suppliers and customers, potentially from other industries. Announcements concerning a particular company, such as earnings or credit rating announcements, tend to affect the stock price of that company as well as stock prices of the firm's competitors or comparable companies. Sudden price run-ups and run-downs in any given security may spill over into prices of related securities.

Most phenomena have the highest impact on security prices around the time of their occurrence. For example, macroeconomic news causes the most significant price disturbances around the time of a news release. Similarly, corporate earnings announcements move securities prices most around the time the earnings are announced.

The expectation of an announcement itself can cause changes to the price of a security. As the time to an announcement shortens, speculation on the direction of the announcement can be driven by unexpected commentaries in the media or the actions of speculators.

Many phenomena driving market prices occur on a schedule. The dates and times of macroeconomic announcements, for example, are known well in advance. As a result, anticipating macroeconomic events and their impact enables quantitative investors to make shrewd portfolio allocations around the event announcement times.

Other phenomena, such as firm-specific credit rating upgrades and downgrades, sudden price run-ups, statistical correlations, and other similar events, can be unpredictable in advance. Many quant investors carefully watch the markets and parse news sources to quickly identify a phenomenon when it occurs.

How Much Money Can be Invested With Each Strategy?

As a rule, the more capital is used in a particular strategy, the smaller the return of the strategy. The maximum level of capital that can be used by the investment strategy without significantly diluting its performance is known as "strategy capacity."

The capacity of each strategy can be determined by a variety of factors, among them regulatory, market, and others. According to the regulations by the U.S. Securities and Exchange Commission (the SEC), for example, one needs to apply for a special registration when holding 5 percent or more of any U.S. stock. The registration process can be cumbersome, and many investors instead limit capacities of their strategies to less than 5 percent of any U.S. company.

Average volume or "liquidity" of a particular security can also determine the capacity of the investment strategy in that security. For example, in foreign exchange, it is customary to trade in blocks of at least $10 million per trade, allowing large capacities for investment strategies. On the other hand, selected options have very small trade sizes and trade very infrequently, limiting strategy capacities.

The capacity of a given strategy may change over time as other investors decide to enter or leave similar strategies, saturating or opening up strategy profitability. To ensure long-term viability of their strategies, most investors continue to research and tweak their strategies over the lifetime of each strategy. Keeping their strategies and tweaks secret also helps to preserve the capacity of their strategies.

A trader running a number of strategies is also aware of the deployment of capital at any time. The frequency of trades across different strategies affects the overall use of capital. Not all quant strategies are intended to capture value at the same pace, and this affects how much capital can be allocated to any given strategy.

How Long Do They Last?

Many quantitative strategies, such as those based on technical analysis and common macroeconomic events, have been around since the 1920s and 1960s. Some strategies appear to last forever, while others lose their potency after five to seven years, yet rebound after additional time passes by.

What Strategies Are Covered in This Almanac?

The Quant Investor Almanac 2011 purposefully avoids complex mathematical constructs and is designed to act as a guide to tried-and-true investment strategies. The strategies covered here include the following investment ideas:

- Event-based strategies, accompanied by a calendar of economic news releases.
- Security-specific strategies, namely, strategies for the following instruments:
  - Stocks (equity)
  - Mutual funds
  - Bonds (fixed income)
  - Currencies (foreign exchange)
  - Exchange-traded funds (ETFs)
  - Futures
  - Options

Event-based strategies describe past responses of prices of different securities to each event, as well as the economic rationale for the event strategy impact on individual financial instruments. Security-specific strategies are derived from the latest top-quality research in finance and include specific investment ideas.

How To Invest

Like most other investing methodologies, quantitative investing works along the following three steps.

1. Determine the target price for each security. The target price can be the output of one or many quantitative investment strategies. It is the expected fair market price of the financial security given all available news and market variables. It is assumed that based on the investor's analysis, the market price for a given security will reach its target price level within the investor's investment horizon.

2. Answer the following question: Given the target price level of the security resulting from Step 1 above, is the security overpriced (too expensive) or underpriced (too cheap) at present? The answer should take into account all transaction costs, including broker and exchange

fees, taxes, opportunity costs, and latent costs such as bid-ask spreads. If the security is deemed underpriced relative to its target price, for example, and the costs of trading are smaller than the potential gain, then a buy-and-hold strategy may be in order.

3. If the strategy is deemed profitable even with trading costs taken into account, put money behind it. If a security is deemed underpriced (overpriced), buy (short-sell) a unit of the security and hold the position until the security price reaches its target level predicted by the quantitative investment model, the holding horizon expires, or the risk-management framework kicks in.

MANAGING RISK

Quant investment strategies identify a future expected value of a security based on a theoretical prediction or an empirical observation. At times, however, predictions fail to materialize and risk management function needs to step in to curtail possible losses.

Like other investment operations, quantitative investing faces these five types of risk:

1. Market risk
2. Credit and counterparty risk
3. Liquidity risk
4. Operational risk
5. Legal risk

Market risk is the risk of a declining net asset value as a result of normal market movements. Market risk is most often expressed as a probability and a dollar value of a possible loss. This type of risk can be mitigated with simple tools, such as stop-loss orders, and more complex mechanisms like hedging. A stop-loss order is an order to close a position the value of which has declined below a pre-specified threshold. A stop-loss order can be placed at the time a position is first opened. Hedging involves finding and investing into a security with risk/return characteristics complementary to the original security to augment the risk profile of the quantitative strategy. For example, if the quantitative investor's main strategy involves going long in (buying) IBM, a simultaneous purchase of IBM put options (rights to sell the IBM stock at a pre-specified price) limits investor's exposure should IBM stock fall.

Credit and counterparty risk for most quantitative investors describes the risk an investor faces if his counterparty—a brokerage or exchange—goes bankrupt or refuses to honor their obligations for some different reason. Thoroughly vetting a counterparty prior to entrusting them with transactions help to mitigate this risk.

Liquidity risk refers to the risk of inability to close (liquidate) investor's positions at a desired price or altogether. Inability to close positions at a desired price may arise in fast-paced trending markets. Inability to close positions altogether can happen in times of crisis when markets fail or shut down. Close monitoring of market conditions and using market orders to close positions helps to alleviate liquidity risk.

Operational risk addresses the risks of losses due to operational malfunctions. For example, failure to comply with governmental regulations is likely to result in fines or stiffer penalties, while errors in placing orders may cost significant money in transaction costs required to remedy the incurred mistakes. Paying close attention to all facets of quantitative investing and staying on top of the latest developments in the industry helps alleviate this type of risk.

Finally, legal risk is the risk of losses due to legal actions. Monitoring one's contractual obligations, reading the fine print, and consulting one's attorney when in doubt may help ease the burden of this type of risk.

WHICH TYPES OF ORDERS ARE BEST FOR QUANT INVESTORS?

Today's investors face a wide array of choices of trading orders. While many innovative orders have been developed to attract traders, basic market and limit orders are still among the most popular order types.

A market order is the most common order type that guarantees execution at the current market price. The price at which the market order ends up executed is not guaranteed. Often, the market price moves in the adverse direction between the time the order is placed and the time the order is executed, resulting in lower-than-expected profitability of market orders.

A limit order is an order to buy or sell at a pre-specified price. Unlike market orders, limit orders are executed at a guaranteed price, but their execution does not necessarily materialize—a limit order is only executed when the market price is the same or better than that of the limit order. Limit orders can be specified to be valid only until a specific date and time. Limit orders can also be cancelled before their expiration. Some exchanges charge fees for cancellations of limit orders.

The investor's optimal choice between a limit and a market order ultimately depends on these key characteristics:

- The investor's ability to monitor the markets throughout the day.
- The investor's urgency to execute a specific order.

Juhani T. Linnainmaa of the University of Chicago (*Journal of Finance*, 2010) has found that limit orders may hurt investors who do not have the opportunity to frequently monitor and adjust their portfolios. Specifically, investors using limit orders, yet having no ability to monitor the markets and cancel their limit orders in a timely fashion, may be "run over" by the markets. The following is an example of a run-over: An investor predicts that a share of IBM stock will rise to $60 from the current level of $50. The investor sets a good-till-cancel limit order to buy several shares of IBM at $47 per share, to capture the upside natural volatility of IBM shares. Several days after the investor places his limit order, however, an unexpected macroeconomic news announcement causes the price of IBM to drop to $35. The investor's limit order is triggered, purchasing stock of IBM at $47 per share, leaving the investor holding a loss of $12 per share ($47 − $35 = $12).

For those investors able to actively monitor their positions, however, limit orders may prove attractive. Entering a long (buy) position using a limit order with a price set a notch below the current market price, for example, allows the investor to take advantage of short-term market volatility and capture a price more attractive than the one feasible if the investor were to use a market order instead. Similarly, entering a short (sell) position using a limit order with the sell price set just above the current market price allows the investor to lock in a tad more profitability due to the normal market oscillations. Limit orders with prices far away from the current market price may result in even greater profitability, but may also take longer to execute or fail to execute altogether, resulting in lost investment opportunities.

THE COSTS OF QUANT INVESTING

A successful quantitative investor maximizes his profitability through obtaining the highest possible returns per unit of risk, all while paying the lowest costs for the quality of execution services required. The execution costs faced by a quantitative investor can be non-trivial; in addition to the most transparent transaction costs, such as the broker's fee per trade, the investor often faces a range of other, latent execution costs. Table 1 provides a high-level overview of the execution costs frequently encountered by quantitative investors.

HOW TO USE THIS ALMANAC

The Almanac offers the reader a timely account of selected quantitative strategies. Among the strategies presented here are the latest cutting-edge strategies developed in the financial academic and practitioner circles.

Many strategies shown are event-based; they describe the behavior of financial instruments around event announcement dates. The events discussed in the Almanac recur on a schedule shown in the calendar pages. Some events occur weekly, while others take place only quarterly. In the calendar, icons accompanying each event indicate which section contains the description of the event in the Almanac.

Table 1 Execution Cost Types and Descriptions

Execution Cost Type	Description
Transparent Execution Costs	
Broker Commissions	Broker commissions cover brokers' costs of business and contain fixed and variable components. Variable cost components are usually set for different levels of transaction volume: The higher the investor volume, the lower the cost per unit of security traded, the higher the brokers' revenues.
Exchange Fees	Exchanges charge fees for matching buy and sell orders on their platforms. Market orders may be more expensive than limit orders as exchanges view limit orders as adding valuable liquidity, while market orders consume exchange liquidity.
Taxes	Quantitative investments of one year or more fall under the reduced taxation category of "capital gains tax" in most jurisdictions. Shorter-term investments are taxed at the regular income tax rate.
Latent Execution Costs	
Bid-Ask Spread	From a quantitative investor's point of view, the bid-ask spread is an additional cost of a round-trip transaction. The bid-ask spread is not known with precision before the investment is made: The spread depends on market condition and changes with time. The likely bid-ask spread can be estimated, however, from past historical data.
Investment Delay	The cost of investment delay is the adverse move of the market incurred by the investor between the time the market order is placed and the market order is executed. It is also known as a latency cost.
Price Appreciation	The cost of price appreciation is the adverse move of the market price a quantitative investor may encounter while executing a large order. Some large orders need to be "sliced" into smaller components; each component may be incrementally more expensive to execute.
Market Impact	The cost of market impact measures the adverse change in the market price *after* the quant investor executes a market order and before he executes another market order in the same security. Most often, the change in price is due to temporary liquidity shortages.
Timing Risk	The cost of timing risk is the loss of value associated with "timing the market"—waiting for the optimal time to enter a position.
Opportunity Cost	The opportunity cost is the gain in other unexecuted investment strategies, forgone in favor of the current quant strategy.

To use the Almanac to its maximum advantage, we recommend the following six steps.

1. Read through all the strategies in the Almanac.

2. Select strategies that appeal to you, based on familiarity with the subject, personal interests, or other reasons.

3. Take time to familiarize yourself with the strategies and their timelines.

4. Track the strategy on paper ("paper-trade") for some time, ensuring that you are comfortable with the hypothetical results the strategy would produce if you were trading real money.

5. Measure the risks you observe, and develop a risk-management framework. The framework can include simple stop-losses and complex rule-based liquidation algorithms.

6. Once you are satisfied with the paper-trading stage, and are comfortable with your assessment of strategy risks, apply the strategy to real capital.

Good luck!

NEW IDEAS IN QUANT INVESTING STRATEGIES: STOCKS

2011 JANUARY

Sun	Mon	Tue	Wed	Thu	Fri	Sat
						1
2	3	4	5	6	7	8
9	10	11	12	13	14	15
16	17	18	19	20	21	22
23	24	25	26	27	28	29
30	31					

KEY HIGHLIGHTS

For the New Year, what's new in stock investing?

- Can Stock Trading Volume and Liquidity Predict Stock Returns?
- Investors Treating Stocks like Lottery Tickets Tend to Lose
- "Overvalued" Equities Can Be Good Investments
- When a Recession Looms, Bank Stocks Are Among the First to Suffer
- International Diversification Still Works, and Works Well

15

CAN STOCK TRADING VOLUME AND
LIQUIDITY PREDICT STOCK RETURNS?

Many non-quantitative equity analysts or "chartists" incorporate stock volume as predictors of future stock prices. Does quantitative investing consider volume and liquidity as predictive variables, and if so, how?

Trading volume measures the cumulative size of all trades completed in a particular financial instrument. According to Simon Gervais, Ron Kaniel, and Dan Mingelgrin (*Journal of Finance*, 2001), stock volume serves as a quantitative predictor of future stock returns for an interesting reason. High stock volume increases the visibility of a particular stock and attracts new investors, whose demand in turn raises the stock price.

Market liquidity is a close cousin of trading volume. Liquidity is a measure of how many buyers and sellers are present in the market at any given time. According to the latest research of Randi Næs, Johannes A. Skjeltorp and Bernt Arne Ødegaard (*Journal of Finance*, 2010), low liquidity often precedes recessions and market crashes. The authors hypothesize that when a recession or a market crash is in the cards, advanced investors leave the markets in a phenomenon known as a "flight to quality."

Changes in trading volume and liquidity, however, can be caused by a variety of factors. One of these factors is risk: Companies facing a higher degree of uncertainty may have stocks trading with a higher volume. These riskier stocks may include growth stocks as well as stocks reacting to adverse news. Another driver of trading volume and liquidity can be a change in the attention a company receives in the press. Stocks with a lot of press coverage tend to incorporate news faster than stocks with low publicity. Yet, according to a study by Lily Fang and Joel Peress (*Journal of Finance*, 2009), stocks with no media coverage tend to deliver higher returns than stocks with ample publicity.

Yet, publicity and trading volume have a complicated quantitative relationship. Publicity resulting from higher volume tends to raise stock prices, while high volume resulting from publicity depresses long-term stock returns. Investors need to exercise caution and due diligence in assessing the causes of high volume and liquidity prior to buying or selling stocks.

JANUARY 3–9, 2011

Events this week:

- Pending Home Sales Index
- Challenger, Gray & Christmas Employment Report
- Unit Auto and Truck Sales for December 2010
- Job Opening and Labor Turnover Survey (JOLTS)
- Manufacturers' Shipments, Inventories, and Orders for November 2010

Monday, January 3, 2011

New Year's Day, observed (Markets Closed)

Tuesday, January 4, 2011

🛒	7:45 A.M.	ICSC Retail Sales Index
🛒	8:55 A.M.	Johnson Redbook Report
⊕	10:00 A.M.	ISM Report on Business—Manufacturing for December 2010
🏠	10:00 A.M.	Construction Spending for November 2010
🛒	5:00 P.M.	ABC News Consumer Comfort Index

Wednesday, January 5, 2011

🏠	7:00 A.M.	U.S. Mortgage Application Indexes
💼	8:15 A.M.	ADP National Employment Report

Thursday, January 6, 2011

💼	6:00 A.M.	Monster Employment Index
💼	8:30 A.M.	U.S. Unemployment Insurance Claims
⊕	10:00 A.M.	ISM Report on Business—Non-Manufacturing for December 2010
💵	11:00 A.M.	13- and 26-Week U.S. T-Bill Auction Announcements
📈	4:30 P.M.	U.S. Monetary Aggregates
📈	4:30 P.M.	U.S. Monetary Base

Friday, January 7, 2011

💼	8:30 A.M.	The Employment Situation

Notes: _____

INVESTORS TREATING STOCKS LIKE
LOTTERY TICKETS TEND TO LOSE

Do you believe that a particular stock may bring you luck? It may be a good time to stop. According to research by Alok Kumar, published in the *Journal of Finance* in 2009, investors with a lottery approach to stocks significantly underperform those with a more scientific approach to choosing equities.

Kumar examines stocks with characteristics similar to the simplest state lotteries that have the following traits.

- Lottery tickets cost little relative to the lottery's jackpot (low price to potential payoff ratio).
- Probability of winning a jackpot is very low.
- The value of the jackpot varies highly from one lottery to the next (the payoff is very risky).
- The average returns on lottery tickets are mildly negative.

In the hunt for lottery-like stocks, stock market gamblers search for lottery characteristics against the entire stock universe. Kumar conjectures that gamblers are mostly looking for cheap bets, and are likely to find low cost stocks (penny stocks) attractive. Furthermore, gamblers are seeking stocks with low prices and high volatility, so that despite much likelihood of a loss, there exists some probability of a very high gain. As a result, gamblers focus on stocks with the following features: high volatility pertaining to the stock only (independent of the market); stock tendency to end up with a negative return; and low stock price.

The author of the study finds that individuals are much more prone to gamble than professional investors. The percent of individual (retail) investors' aggregate wealth invested in lottery stocks is 3.74 percent, and only 0.76 percent of professional investors' money is allocated to lottery equities.

Furthermore, it turns out that investors who allocate at least one-third of their total investable wealth to lottery stocks on average lose at least 2.5 percent per year, after adjusting for risk. A typical investor who gambles a part of his portfolio can improve his performance by over 2.8 percent per year just by reallocating his stock gambling capital to non-lottery stocks.

JANUARY 10–16, 2011

Events this week:

- Bank of Canada Target Bank Rate Announcement
- NFIB Small Business Optimism Index for December 2010
- U.S. Industrial Production and Capacity Utilization for December 2010
- U.S. Retail Sales for December 2010
- Manufacturing and Trade Inventories and Sales for November 2010
- Treasury International Capital Flows for November 2010
- Consumer Price Index
- Producer Price Index
- Housing Starts and Building Permits for December 2010
- International Trade Balance for November 2010
- Job Opening and Labor Turnover Survey (JOLTS)
- Import and Export Prices
- Productivity and Costs

Monday, January 10, 2011

Adults' Day (Japan Markets Closed)

11:00 A.M. U.S. Treasury Bill Auction Announcement

Tuesday, January 11, 2011

7:45 A.M. ICSC Retail Sales Index

8:55 A.M. Johnson Redbook Report

5:00 P.M. ABC News Consumer Comfort Index

Wednesday, January 12, 2011

7:00 A.M. U.S. Mortgage Application Indexes

2:00 P.M. U.S. Federal Budget Balance

2:00 P.M. Current Economic Conditions ("Beige Book")

Thursday, January 13, 2011

7:00 A.M. Bank of England Rate Decision

7:45 A.M. European Central Bank Interest Rate Announcement

8:30 A.M. U.S. Unemployment Insurance Claims

11:00 A.M. 13- and 26-Week U.S. T-Bill Auction Announcements

4:30 P.M. U.S. Monetary Aggregates

4:30 P.M. U.S. Monetary Base

Friday, January 14, 2011

10:00 A.M. U.S. Consumer Sentiment, preliminary data

Notes:

"OVERVALUED" EQUITIES CAN BE
GOOD INVESTMENTS

The "fair price" of a stock is in the eyes of the beholder. Investors base their equity pricing on various approaches, including but not limited to technical analysis, fundamental analysis, or a variety of other more and less quantitative techniques. The outcome of such pricing is always the same: If a stock is deemed overpriced, a sell order is placed, while a stock that is lower than the model's prediction is bought with the expectation that the price will rise to its assessed fair value.

In reaching conclusions on whether stocks are overvalued, many traders and analysts take into account growth prospects of the firms under consideration. Firms facing few organic growth prospects with stocks priced above those of their peers are often considered overvalued.

New research shows, however, that seemingly overvalued firms frequently find outlets for strong nonorganic growth. In a June 2009 *Journal of Finance* article, Pavel Savor and Qi Lu, of the Wharton School and Kellogg School, respectively, argue that stocks deemed overvalued by conventional measures are naturally bound to grow through acquiring other firms, and specifically by paying with their own stock, not cash. According to Savor and Lu, the firms that are deemed overvalued, yet are able to successfully complete a stock-for-firm acquisition, fare much better in subsequent years than do firms that are deemed overvalued but failed to acquire other firms using their stock. If a firm seems to be overvalued, an investor should consider the likelihood that it will make a successful acquisition; if so, the firm's stock may be attractively priced.

Rather than relying on company growth prospects, another team of researchers recommends looking at the volatility of the firm's cash flows in valuing the company's stock. Randolph Cohen, Christopher Polk, and Tuomo Vuolteenaho (*Journal of Finance*, December 2009) find that firms with strong and consistent cash flows significantly outperform firms with weak or volatile cash flows over 5- and even 15-year investment horizons.

In reaching their conclusions, the authors of the study considered various potential predictors: prior monthly and annual stock returns, a proportion of the firm's balance sheet allocated to debt, relative changes in

JANUARY 17–23, 2011

Events this week:

- Bank of Canada Target Bank Rate Announcement
- U.S. Durable Goods Orders for December 2010
- Composite Index of Leading Economic Indicators for December 2010
- Housing Starts and Building Permits for December 2010

Monday, January 17, 2011

Martin Luther King Day (U.S. Markets Closed)

Tuesday, January 18, 2011

🛒	**7:45 A.M.**	ICSC Retail Sales Index
🔧	**8:30 A.M.**	Empire State Manufacturing Survey
🛒	**8:55 A.M.**	Johnson Redbook Report
🔧	**10:00 A.M.**	ISM Report on Manufacturing
🛒	**5:00 P.M.**	ABC News Consumer Comfort Index

Wednesday, January 19, 2011

🏠	**7:00 A.M.**	U.S. Mortgage Application Indexes

Thursday, January 20, 2011

💼	**8:30 A.M.**	U.S. Unemployment Insurance Claims
🔧	**10:00 A.M.**	Philadelphia Fed Business Outlook Survey
💰	**11:00 A.M.**	13- and 26-Week U.S. T-Bill Auction Announcements
📈	**4:30 P.M.**	U.S. Monetary Aggregates
📈	**4:30 P.M.**	U.S. Monetary Base

Friday, January 21, 2011

📊	**12:00 P.M.**	January 2011 options expire

Notes:

the firm's accounting assets, and stock riskiness with respect to that of the markets. The size and stability of the firm's cash flows proved to be the most significant factor behind predictions of stock prices in the long run.

WHEN A RECESSION LOOMS, BANK STOCKS ARE AMONG THE FIRST TO SUFFER

When a recession hits a particular sector of the economy, most companies within that sector begin to feel the pain. Shrunken prospects of one firm often signify bad news and lower the stock prices for their peer group. As some firms default, so do the others.

The infectious spread of corporate defaults is known as "default clustering" or "credit contagion." It is often overlooked in equity pricing, and may have accounted for a fair share of risk miscalculations resulting in the credit crisis of 2007–2008.

Credit contagion is useful to consider when pricing all stocks, and not just those in the industry most affected by the recession. When companies begin to default, they immediately damage their creditors' balance sheets, according to a study by Philippe Jorion and Gaiyan Zhang (*Journal of Finance*, October 2009). Since banks are the primary creditors across industries their prospects and stock prices falter as soon as any corner of the economy falls ill.

Yet, not all credit to industrial firms is extended by banks. Jorion and Zhang point out that industrial firms are also likely to borrow from their suppliers in the form of trade credit. If a firm defaults, its suppliers are likely to feel a financial stress as well, potentially extending contagion to the supplier's industry, and lowering equity prices there.

As a result, when valuing equities, pay attention to the credit relationships of the firm. When credit data of a specific firm is not available, data on the company's industry peers should be used to establish the financial exposure and the health of the firm.

Understanding the nature of a firm's clientele is equally important. If a firm's clients are spread out across the country or in various industries, it

JANUARY 24–30, 2011

Events this week:

- Advance GDP figures, fourth quarter 2010, U.S.
- Advance Personal Income, fourth quarter 2010, U.S.
- U.S. Durable Goods Orders for December 2010
- Manufacturers' Shipments, Inventories, and Orders for December 2010
- Personal Consumption Expenditures for December 2010
- PCE- and GDP-Based Price Indexes for December 2010
- Employment Cost Index for fourth quarter 2010

Monday, January 24, 2011

11:00 A.M.   U.S. Treasury Bill Auction Announcement

Tuesday, January 25, 2011

7:45 A.M.   ICSC Retail Sales Index

8:55 A.M.   Johnson Redbook Report

9:00 A.M.   S&P/Case Schiller Home Price Indexes for December 2010

10:00 A.M.   Consumer Confidence (Conference Board)

10:00 A.M.   Richmond Federal Reserve Bank Survey for December 2010

10:00 A.M.   Existing Home Sales for December 2010

5:00 P.M.   ABC News Consumer Comfort Index

Wednesday, January 26, 2011

7:00 A.M.   U.S. Mortgage Application Indexes

7:00 A.M.   Bank of England Minutes of the Monetary Policy Committee (U.K.)

Thursday, January 27, 2011

8:30 A.M.   U.S. Unemployment Insurance Claims

10:00 A.M.   Help Wanted Advertising Index for December 2010

11:00 A.M.   Kansas City Federal Reserve Bank Manufacturing Survey for December 2010

11:00 A.M.   13- and 26-Week U.S. T-Bill Auction Announcements

4:30 P.M.   U.S. Monetary Aggregates

4:30 P.M.   Monetary Base

Friday, January 28, 2011

10:00 A.M.   U.S. Consumer Sentiment, final data

Notes:

is more likely to weather a storm should one or several of their customers default. On the other hand, firms with one or a few large customers heavily concentrated in specific industries are more likely to experience financial distress as a result of their customers' ills. The same applies to banks and other financial lenders: Well-diversified institutions are more likely to weather their customer crises than smaller specialized outfits targeting niche industries and having a limited array of borrowers.

INTERNATIONAL DIVERSIFICATION STILL WORKS, AND WORKS WELL

Classical financial theory recommends diversification of assets as a means to reduce risk (volatility) in one's portfolio. To successfully diversify a portfolio, an investor needs to combine stocks with returns exhibiting the least co-movement or correlation.

What stocks are more likely to have low correlation? Prices of stocks driven by different events tend to exhibit less correlation than stocks driven by the same occurrences. Stocks in disparate industries, for example, are often less correlated than stocks in the same industry, as the latter are prone to have similar responses to events, such as supply shocks. According to new research by Geert Bekaert, Robert Hodrick, and Xiaoyan Zhang (*Journal of Finance*, December 2009), stocks trading in different countries are also not very well correlated and are good candidates for diversifying one's portfolio.

While one can buy a Big Mac virtually everywhere, stock markets appear to remain at the same level of global integration as they were 10 years ago. According to the authors of the study, stock markets in different international jurisdictions seldom move in the same direction, even in the today's globalized environment. Advances in U.S. stocks do not translate into rising prices in Europe or Asia, for example.

The lack of correlation across international stock markets can be partially explained by differences in the types of companies that are listed across the globe. Bekaert and his co-authors note that the average size of a publicly traded firm in Japan is $1,538 million, while it is only $218 million in Greece.

JANUARY 31–FEBRUARY 6, 2011

Events this week:

- Pending Home Sales, U.S.
- Challenger, Gray & Christmas Employment Report
- Manufacturers' Shipments, Inventories, and Orders for December 2010
- Consumer Credit for December 2010
- Housing Vacancies and Homeownership Rates

Monday, January 31, 2011

9:45 A.M. Chicago Business Barometer

11:00 A.M. U.S. Treasury Bill Auction Announcement

Notes: _____

Furthermore, the authors of the study detect few trends in stock cor-relations across various markets. That is, stock correlations do not appear to persistently change much over time. The only exception to this observation is the interrelation of the European markets: Those exhibit more and more correlation, probably under the effect of the increasingly cohesive regula-tory regime across Europe.

In short, stocks in different regions of the world present attractive diversification benefits for investors' portfolios. And as many brokerages offer increasingly seamless trading connections to various international exchanges, accessing foreign markets and diversifying using foreign stocks has never been easier.

CUTTING-EDGE QUANT INVESTING STRATEGIES: FOREIGN EXCHANGE, MUTUAL FUNDS, AND ETFs

FEBRUARY 2011

Sun	Mon	Tue	Wed	Thu	Fri	Sat
		1	2	3	4	5
6	7	8	9	10	11	12
13	14	15	16	17	18	19
20	21	22	23	24	25	26
27	28					

KEY HIGHLIGHTS

February is a good time to pay your holiday bills and invest your bonus. This month brings you some new thinking on diversifying your investments.

- Trading ETFs on Correlation Risk
- Foreign Exchange Is an Investable Asset, Too
- Using Foreign Currencies to Hedge Equity Portfolios
- Investing in a 401(k)? Avoid Your Company's Trustees
- What Is the Best Way to Allocate Your 401(k) Investments?

TRADING ETFs ON CORRELATION RISK

Correlation is a measure of how closely changes in prices, or returns, of two or more securities move together over time. If any two stocks rise and fall in tandem, their returns show strong positive correlation. If any two stocks consistently move in opposite directions relative to each other (one stock rises whenever another stock falls), the returns of these stocks exhibit strong negative correlation. If prices of two stocks move independently from one another, their correlation is said to be small or near zero.

Pairs of stocks that are rising, yet exhibit negative or no correlation with each other, provide additional benefit to their investors: portfolio diversification. Portfolio diversification is often described in colloquial terms as spreading one's nest eggs among several baskets. Should one basket that is invested in one stock drop (and crack), eggs in another basket will stay whole, providing the baskets are negatively correlated or uncorrelated. If both baskets move in tandem, both will drop at the same time, destroying all of the eggs. Thus, diversification among several negatively correlated or uncorrelated baskets reduces the risk of the overall investment. Many passive mutual funds and exchange-traded funds (ETFs) have been developed to take advantage of this diversification principle. For the price of one share of a single stock, passive mutual funds and ETFs claim to provide investors reduced investment risk through diversification.

Stock return correlations are typically estimated by observing the behavior of selected stocks every day over a finite period of time, such as a year or a month. Correlations, however, change over time. In particular, when equity markets gradually rise, some stocks rise while others do not. Yet, when equity markets crash, most of the stocks fall together. That is, when equity markets crash, correlations of all stock returns increase (become more positive).

As a result, during periods of market crashes, mutual funds and ETFs become particularly risky investments, often much riskier than the underlying individual stocks. A natural "crash" trading strategy arises: When markets crash, sell mutual funds and ETFs and buy individual stocks with strong fundamental values. Such a strategy can be considered a fundamentals-based concentration strategy: Decrease portfolio diversification, i.e., decrease holdings of indexes and ETFs, and increase holdings of individual stocks during the crash times when the benefits of diversification are limited.

Events this week:

- Pending Home Sales, U.S.
- Challenger, Gray & Christmas Employment Report
- Unit Auto and Truck Sales for January 2011
- Housing Vacancies and Homeownership Rates
- Job Opening and Labor Turnover Survey (JOLTS)

Tuesday, February 1, 2011

Notes: _____

🛒	7:45 A.M.	ICSC Retail Sales Index
🛒	8:55 A.M.	Johnson Redbook Report
⚙	10:00 A.M.	ISM Report on Business—Manufacturing for January 2011
🏠	10:00 A.M.	Construction Spending for December 2010
🛒	5:00 P.M.	ABC News Consumer Comfort Index

Wednesday, February 2, 2011

🏠	7:00 A.M.	U.S. Mortgage Application Indexes
💼	8:15 A.M.	ADP National Employment Report

Thursday, February 3, 2011

💼	6:00 A.M.	Monster Employment Index
💰	7:45 A.M.	European Central Bank Interest Rate Announcement
💼	8:30 A.M.	U.S. Unemployment Insurance Claims
⚙	10:00 A.M.	ISM Report on Business—Non-Manufacturing for January 2011
🏠	10:00 A.M.	OFHEO Home Price Index, U.S.
💰	11:00 A.M.	13- and 26-Week U.S. T-Bill Auction Announcements
📈	4:30 P.M.	U.S. Monetary Aggregates
📈	4:30 P.M.	U.S. Monetary Base

Friday, February 4, 2011

💼	8:30 A.M.	The Employment Situation

As an example, let's consider the price behavior of SPY, an ETF tracking the S&P 500, and a couple of its randomly selected long-time constituents, 3M Company (MMM) and Abbott Laboratories (ABT). Following each extreme negative day in SPY during 2007–2009, SPY rose slightly, yet both MMM and ABT rose more. Following each extreme positive day in SPY during 2007–2009, SPY fell on average, yet MMM and ABT did not clearly follow suit: MMM fell less than SPY, and ABT fell more. The same behavior accompanies other constituents of the S&P 500 as documented in Aldridge and Krawciw (2010), paving the way for a concentration strategy following dramatic negative events in equity markets.

Diversification of stocks works only when correlations are low. When correlations are high, concentration becomes a better strategy.

FOREIGN EXCHANGE IS AN INVESTABLE ASSET, TOO

Ask an average investor what associations come to mind on foreign exchange, and you will hear of trips abroad and different-looking coins found there. Yet, foreign exchange can be thought of and invested in just like equities and bonds. In fact, foreign exchange can provide investors valuable international diversification, enhancing the return of their portfolios while minimizing risk of overall portfolio.

Foreign exchange is widely traded. Unlike stocks and bonds, foreign exchange securities (known as foreign exchange pairs) and foreign exchange markets have the following three properties:

1. Foreign exchange lacks a centralized trading venue. While many stocks, futures, and options are traded on centralized exchanges, foreign exchange trades through loose associations of broker-dealers, known as inter-dealer networks. As a result, foreign exchange rates do not have a single price: Several records of a foreign exchange price can be available at any given moment, each slightly varying from the next.

2. Foreign exchange values can never drop to zero. Foreign exchange pairs can never go bankrupt (even if a country defaults on its debt), unlike prices of equities and other common financial instruments. Even when one

Events this week:

- U.S. NFIB Small Business Optimism Index for January 2011
- U.S. Manufacturing and Trade Inventories and Sales for December 2010
- International Trade Balance for December 2010
- Job Opening and Labor Turnover Survey (JOLTS)
- Consumer Price Index
- Productivity and Costs
- Import and Export Prices

Monday, February 7, 2011

11:00 A.M.   U.S. Treasury Bill Auction Announcement

Tuesday, February 8, 2011

7:45 A.M.   ICSC Retail Sales Index

8:55 A.M.   Johnson Redbook Report

5:00 P.M.   ABC News Consumer Comfort Index

Wednesday, February 9, 2011

7:00 A.M.   U.S. Mortgage Application Indexes

Thursday, February 10, 2011

7:00 A.M.   Bank of England Rate Decision (U.K.)

8:30 A.M.   U.S. Unemployment Insurance Claims

11:00 A.M.   13- and 26-Week U.S. T-Bill Auction Announcements

2:00 P.M.   U.S. Federal Budget Balance

4:30 P.M.   U.S. Monetary Aggregates

4:30 P.M.   U.S. Monetary Base

Friday, February 11, 2011

National Foundation Day (Japan Markets Closed)

10:00 A.M.   U.S. Consumer Sentiment, preliminary data

Notes: _____

country's currency is significantly weaker than the currency of another country, the value of the exchange rate between the two countries will always be either very large or very small, but never zero.

3. Foreign exchange markets are scarcely regulated and investors should be cautious of "too-good-to-be-true" offers from unscrupulous dealers.

In light of the unique properties of foreign exchange rates, investing in foreign currencies may be uncomfortable to many investors. In reality, many brokerages now offer their clients the ability to buy and hold foreign exchange in their accounts, alongside stocks. Just holding a basket of various foreign currencies in your portfolio diversifies the risk of your portfolio's exposure to domestic markets; should S&P 500 unexpectedly fall, selected currencies may rise, propping up your portfolio.

Using Foreign Currencies to Hedge Equity Portfolios

One application of foreign currency helps to mitigate the risks of other investments denominated in the same currency. As usual, to diversify a portfolio of securities, a quant investor seeks to buy (long) a security that has the most negative correlation with the original portfolio, and to sell (short) a security that has a positive correlation with the portfolio.*

An all-equity portfolio denominated in U.S. dollars is positively correlated with the U.S. dollar itself. That is, when the U.S. dollar rises against the Euro, the aggregate value of the U.S.-denominated equity portfolio also rises against the Euro, in tandem with the U.S. dollar. To optimize a U.S. equity portfolio, an investor can short the U.S. dollar by buying and holding Euros. (Note that the opposite logic applies to diversification of bond portfolios. The U.S. dollar, for example, tends to rise when bond prices fall and vice versa.)

Buying just one foreign currency, however, can add significant risk associated with the country of that currency. To manage this problem, an

---

*A positive (negative) correlation of the portfolio and a security implies that when the total value of the original portfolio rises, the price of the optimal diversification security rises (falls) at the same time. On the other hand, under positive (negative) correlation, when the aggregate value of the original portfolio falls, the price of the diversifying security falls (rises).

FEBRUARY 14–20, 2011

FEBRUARY

Events this week:

- Composite Index of Leading Economic Indicators for January 2011
- U.S. Retail Sales for January 2011
- U.S. Industrial Production and Capacity Utilization for January 2011
- Housing Starts and Building Permits for January 2011
- Treasury International Capital Flows for December 2010
- Consumer Price Index
- Producer Price Index
- Productivity and Costs

Monday, February 14, 2011

11:00 A.M.   U.S. Treasury Bill Auction Announcement

Tuesday, February 15, 2011

7:45 A.M.   ICSC Retail Sales Index
8:30 A.M.   Empire State Manufacturing Survey
8:55 A.M.   Johnson Redbook Report
5:00 P.M.   ABC News Consumer Comfort Index

Wednesday, February 16, 2011

7:00 A.M.   U.S. Mortgage Application Indexes
7:00 A.M.   Bank of England Inflation Report (U.K.)

Thursday, February 17, 2011

8:30 A.M.   U.S. Unemployment Insurance Claims
10:00 A.M.   Philadelphia Fed Business Outlook Survey Production
11:00 A.M.   13- and 26-Week U.S. T-Bill Auction Announcements
4:30 P.M.   U.S. Monetary Aggregates
4:30 P.M.   U.S. Monetary Base

Friday, February 18, 2011

12:00 P.M.   February 2011 options expire

Notes:

Table 2   Common ETFs

Symbol	Description	Correlation with the S&P 500 (weekly data, 2007–2010)
FXC	Canadian Dollar ETF	59.07%
FXA	Australian Dollar ETF	67.96%
FXE	U.S. Dollar-Euro ETF	32.41%
FXY	Japanese Yen ETF	−47.78%
FXS	Swedish Krona ETF	45.36%

investor can simultaneously short the U.S. dollar against a portfolio or a basket of currencies.

In addition, instead of buying and holding the physical currencies, the investor may choose to hold an ETF "tracking" a given currency pair. Table 2 shows several common ETFs that can be purchased and held just like ordinary stocks.

With the exception of FXY, a proxy for the Japanese yen, other currency ETFs listed above are positively correlated with the S&P 500. Therefore, while a long (buy) position in FXY will diversify a long (buy-and-hold) portfolio of the U.S. stocks, a short (sell) position in FXC, FXA, FXE, or FXS is required to accomplish the same goal.

INVESTING IN A 401(K)? AVOID YOUR COMPANY'S TRUSTEES

Corporate 401(k) retirement plans have become the majority investors in U.S. mutual funds (money markets excluded). According to the Investment Company Institute, the Federal Reserve, and the Department of Labor, total mutual funds assets in the United States in 2004 amounted to $8.1 trillion, of which 40 percent were investments from corporate retirement accounts. By 2006, the share of 401(k) rose to 60 percent of all mutual fund investments.

While the explosive expansion of 401(k) investments has been a boon to mutual fund managers, it has also created conflicts of interest. According to the research of Lauren Cohen and Breno Schmidt (*Journal of Finance,*

Events this week:

- U.S. Durable Goods Orders for January 2011
- Personal Consumption Expenditures for January 2011
- Housing Starts and Building Permits for January 2011

Monday, February 21, 2011

President's Day (U.S. Markets Closed)

Notes: _____

Tuesday, February 22, 2011

7:45 A.M.	ICSC Retail Sales Index
8:55 A.M.	Johnson Redbook Report
9:00 A.M.	S&P/Case-Shiller Home Price Indexes for January 2011
10:00 A.M.	Richmond Federal Reserve Bank Survey for January 2011
10:00 A.M.	Consumer Confidence
5:00 P.M.	ABC News Consumer Comfort Index

Wednesday, February 23, 2011

7:00 A.M. U.S. Mortgage Application Indexes

7:00 A.M. Bank of England Minutes of the Monetary Policy Committee (U.K.)

Thursday, February 24, 2011

8:30 A.M. U.S. Unemployment Insurance Claims

10:00 A.M. Help Wanted Advertising Index for January 2011

11:00 A.M. Kansas City Federal Reserve Bank Manufacturing Survey for January 2011

11:00 A.M. 13- and 26-Week U.S. T-Bill Auction Announcements

4:30 P.M. U.S. Monetary Aggregates

4:30 P.M. U.S. Monetary Base

Friday, February 25, 2011

10:00 A.M. Existing Home Sales for January 2011

10:00 A.M. U.S. Consumer Sentiment, final data

October 2009), some mutual fund managers reward the corporations placing 401(k) assets in a managers' mutual fund by investing disproportionally into the firm's stock. As a result, the mutual fund managers become less objective in their investment goals. This affects other investors into these mutual funds as well as individuals who entrust their retirements to these corporate 401(k) plans.

According to Cohen and Schmidt, mutual fund managers acting as trustees for 401(k) plans of corporations have particularly strong incentives to invest into their corporate clients' stock. On average, trustee funds hold $62 million or 47 percent more of their corporate clients' stock than do mutual funds not bound by trustee relationships. Such a distortion of optimal asset allocations is likely to adversely affect the investment performance of the 401(k) investors.

In a worst-case scenario, the firm falters, employees and 401(k) investors lose jobs, and then the company's stock falls, reducing employees' retirement savings—wiping out years of hard work.

Since most employees lack control over the holdings of a 401(k) program, there is a compelling case for self-directed investments. Yet, many employers do not offer self-directed investing. Even when a self-directed option exists, it can be too time-consuming, as it requires continuous disciplined research. Instead, selecting a mutual fund that does not act as a trustee for any corporation may be the answer to eliminating the moral hazard accompanying many 401(k) allocations.

WHAT IS THE BEST WAY TO ALLOCATE YOUR 401(K) INVESTMENTS?

Most households in the United States have few financial assets outside of their 401(k). Properly managing a 401(k) is the subject of many books, most of which suggest that the prospective investors pay attention to the following factors:

- Projected effect of news on securities and funds.
- Expected returns of individual securities and mutual funds.
- Employer-specific news, such as increased firm-wide stability.

Events this week:

- Preliminary GDP Figures, fourth quarter 2010, U.S.
- Preliminary Personal Income, fourth quarter 2010, U.S.
- Preliminary Corporate Profits, fourth quarter 2010, U.S.
- Pending Home Sales Index
- Challenger, Gray & Christmas Employment Report Employment
- Bank of Canada Target Bank Rate Announcement
- Manufacturers' Shipments, Inventories, and Orders for January 2011
- U.S. Durable Goods Orders for January 2011
- PCE- and GDP-Based Price Indexes for January 2011

Monday, February 28, 2011

9:45 A.M.   Chicago Business Barometer

11:00 A.M.   U.S. Treasury Bill Auction Announcement

Notes:

- Investor goals and risk profile.
- Investor's level of income.

According to new research from James Choi et al. (*Journal of Finance*, December 2009), however, many mutual fund and 401(k) investors ignore best practices when they make investment decisions. Most investors rely too heavily on the previous year's performance of their mutual funds to project the future performance of their funds. For example, investors with an increase in their 401(k) in any given year are likely to allocate more of their money to their 401(k) in the following year, regardless of the composition of their 401(k) portfolios and the performance of markets. Conversely, investors who lost money in their 401(k) accounts one year are likely to decrease their 401(k) allocations in the following year.

According to the researchers, investors whose 401(k) portfolios gained at least 10 percent in any given year are likely to add an additional 0.13 percent of their annual income to their 401(k) by the same year's end. In comparison, a typical investor increases his allocation to a worse-performing 401(k) portfolio by only 0.3 percent of his annual income.

Previous studies documented similar investor behavior. For example, Brad Barber, Terrance Odean, and Michal Strahilevets of the University of California at Berkeley show in their 2004 working paper that investors tend to repurchase stocks they had previously sold for a gain, and avoid stocks that had resulted in losses in their accounts. Ulrike Malmendier and Stefan Nagel of Stanford University (working paper, 2007) detect generational preferences for particular securities: Generations that grew up during periods of high inflation are likely to hold fewer bonds than other generations. These decisions are clearly based more on investor experience than purely on financial analysis.

The reliance on past performance has some statistical rationale. Consider the S&P 500. Of the 59 years from 1950 through 2009, the S&P 500 increased in 43 years and decreased in 16 years. Following the 43 years when the level of the S&P 500 increased, the S&P 500 also increased in the following year 31 times (72 percent of the time). By contrast, following the 16 years when the S&P 500 level declined, the S&P 500 further declined in 4 years (25 percent of the time).

Yet, many researchers believe that such reliance on recurrent behavior is limiting investors' potential to maximize returns because such predictable behavior can be the basis of algorithmic strategies.

NATIONAL OUTPUT AND INCOME

2011

Sun	Mon	Tue	Wed	Thu	Fri	Sat
		1	2	3	4	5
6	7	8	9	10	11	12
13	14	15	16	17	18	19
20	21	22	23	24	25	26
27	28	29	30	31		

KEY HIGHLIGHTS

As the quarter ends, let's review the key quarterly indicators.

- GDP Reports and Their Market Influences
- Gross Private Domestic Investments and the Stock Market
- How Are Individuals Doing?—Personal Income
- Are Corporate Profits a Meaningful Economic Indicator?
- Net Exports and the U.S. Dollar

GDP REPORTS AND THEIR MARKET INFLUENCES

The U.S. Gross Domestic Product (GDP) is a measure of national income. GDP estimates the total value of goods and services produced in the United States in the previous quarter. The U.S. GDP figures are reported by the Department of Commerce at the Bureau of Economic Analysis.

GDP is reported in three stages.

1. Advanced GDP figures for the previous quarter are reported one month after the quarter end.

2. Preliminary GDP is assessed one month after the Advanced GDP is released.

3. Revised GDP comes out one month following Preliminary GDP figures, three months after the quarter end.

GDP is a function of both quantity and prices of goods and services produced on U.S. soil. Prices of goods, however, rise and fall with inflation, and can obscure the true expansions and contractions of economy. To abstract GDP figures from inflation, the Bureau of Economic Analysis

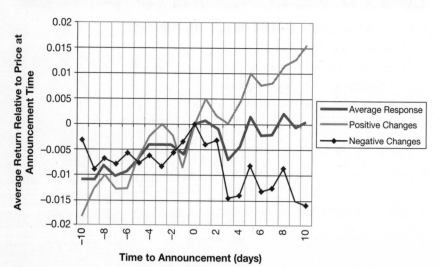

Figure 1   Response of XLU to Changes in U.S. GDP.

Events this week:

- Preliminary GDP Figures, fourth quarter 2010, U.S.
- Preliminary Personal Income, fourth quarter 2010, U.S.
- Preliminary Corporate Profits, fourth quarter 2010, U.S.
- Unit Auto and Truck Sales for February 2011
- Pending Home Sales Index
- Challenger, Gray & Christmas Employment Report
- Manufacturers' Shipments, Inventories and Orders for January 2011
- Personal Consumption Expenditures for January 2011
- Job Opening and Labor Turnover Survey (JOLTS)

FEB/MAR

Tuesday, March 1, 2011

🛒	7:45 A.M.	ICSC Retail Sales Index
🛒	8:55 A.M.	Johnson Redbook Report
⚙	10:00 A.M.	ISM Report on Business—Manufacturing for February 2011
🏠	10:00 A.M.	Construction Spending for January 2011
🛒	5:00 P.M.	ABC News Consumer Comfort Index

Wednesday, March 2, 2011

🏠	7:00 A.M.	U.S. Mortgage Application Indexes
💼	8:15 A.M.	ADP National Employment Report
⚙	2:00 P.M.	Current Economic Conditions ("Beige Book")

Thursday, March 3, 2011

💼	6:00 A.M.	Monster Employment Index
📷	7:45 A.M.	European Central Bank Interest Rate Announcement
💼	8:30 A.M.	U.S. Unemployment Insurance Claims
⚙	10:00 A.M.	ISM Report on Business—Non-Manufacturing for February 2010
📷	11:00 A.M.	13- and 26-Week U.S. T-Bill Auction Announcements
📉	4:30 P.M.	U.S. Monetary Aggregates
📉	4:30 P.M.	U.S. Monetary Base

Friday, March 4, 2011

💼	8:30 A.M.	The Employment Situation

Notes: _____

reports "real" GDP—GDP computed as the index of quantities produced during the latest quarter, and ignoring price increases.

Real GDP is a straightforward measure of economic activity and has a direct impact on U.S. equities. Positive real GDP figures tend to lift the markets, while negative GDP figures depress stocks. Figure 1 (on page 40) shows the average response of one of the U.S. traded equities, Utilities Sector ETF (ticker: XLU). When the announced quarterly Real GDP Seasonally Adjusted Annual Rate (SAAR) figures rise, so does XLU stock. Conversely, when real GDP falls, XLU stock does too. This response is echoed across many U.S. equities.

GROSS PRIVATE DOMESTIC INVESTMENTS AND THE STOCK MARKET

The U.S. Gross Domestic Product (GDP) figures track three major classes of metrics.

- Gross Private Domestic Investment—infusions into the U.S. economy by private corporations.
- Personal Consumption Expenditure—domestic spending of consumers.
- Government Consumption Expenditures and Gross Investment— government spending.

Gross Private Domestic Investment (GPDI) is the fastest growing component of the U.S. GDP. As Figure 2 (on page 44) shows, GPDI has been growing on average by 5.9 percent each quarter since 1947, as compared to the 3.5 percent average quarterly growth in Personal Consumption Expenditure, and 3.3 percent average quarterly growth in Government Consumption Expenditures and Gross Investment.

GPDI comprises both fixed investment from the private sector and investment in working capital (i.e., inventories). Changes in GPDI potentially indicate the private sector's outlook on the economy. Yet, increases in new investments expand the uncertainty of private sector firms—some investments may work out, and some may not. Conversely, a decline in investments reduces the risks of private firms. Accordingly, quarterly

MARCH 7–13, 2011

Events this week:

- U.S. NFIB Small Business Optimism Index for February 2011
- U.S. Industrial Production and Capacity Utilization for February 2011
- U.S. Manufacturing and Trade Inventory and Sales for January 2011
- Housing Market Index
- International Trade Balance for January 2011
- Job Opening and Labor Turnover Survey for January 2011
- Consumer Price Index
- Import & Export Prices
- Flow of Funds
- Manufacturers' Shipments, Inventories and Orders for January 2011
- Job Opening and Labor Turnover Survey (JOLTS)
- Productivity and Costs
- Import and Export Prices

Monday, March 7, 2011

| 11:00 A.M. | U.S. Treasury Bill Auction Announcement |

Tuesday, March 8, 2011

12:01 A.M.	Manpower Employment Outlook Survey
7:45 A.M.	ICSC Retail Sales Index
8:55 A.M.	Johnson Redbook Report
3:00 P.M.	Consumer Credit for January 2011
5:00 P.M.	ABC News Consumer Comfort Index

Wednesday, March 9, 2011

| 7:00 A.M. | U.S. Mortgage Application Indexes |

Thursday, March 10, 2011

6:00 A.M.	Monster Employment Index
7:00 A.M.	Bank of England Rate Decision (U.K.)
8:30 A.M.	U.S. Unemployment Insurance Claims
11:00 A.M.	13- and 26-Week U.S. T-Bill Auction Announcements
2:00 P.M.	U.S. Federal Budget Balance
4:30 P.M.	U.S. Monetary Aggregates
4:30 P.M.	U.S. Monetary Base

Friday, March 11, 2011

| 10:00 A.M. | U.S. Consumer Sentiment, preliminary data |

Notes:

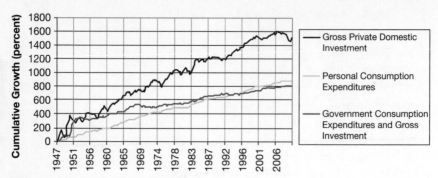

Figure 2   Percent Growth of GDP Components Since 1947.

advances (declines) in GPDI are accompanied by hikes (reductions) in market volatility, as measured by VIX, the index tracking volatility of S&P 500. On average, the week a preliminary rise in GPDI is announced, VIX increases by 1.4 percent, while a preliminary decrease in GPDI tends to lower VIX by 3.2 percent.

This market reaction to GPDI is particularly topical for equity options investors, as prices of both puts and calls on equities increase with advances in market volatility and fall with declines in volatility.

How Are Individuals Doing?— Personal Income

Personal Income (PI) figures are reported monthly, at 8:30 A.M. shortly after GDP releases. PI reports annualize pretax earnings of all non-corporate entities: individuals, private trust funds, and non-for-profit organizations.

The bulk of PI figures (68 percent) come from Labor compensation. Labor compensation in turn comprises wages and salaries (55 percent), followed by "transfer payments," including Social Security and unemployment (15 percent), pensions and insurance benefits (13 percent), individuals' interest income (9 percent), farm and non-farm individual proprietors' income (9 percent), dividends (6 percent), and rental income (1 percent).

Events this week:

- Housing Starts and Building Permits for February 2011
- New Single-Family Home Sales for February 2011
- Current Account Balance, fourth quarter 2010
- Treasury International Capital Flows for January 2011
- Job Opening and Labor Turnover Survey (JOLTS) for January 2011
- Consumer Price Index
- Producer Price Index
- U.S. Industrial Production and Capacity Utilization for February 2011
- U.S. Retail Sales for February 2011
- Composite Index of Leading Economic Indicators for February 2011

MARCH

Monday, March 14, 2011

11:00 A.M.   U.S. Treasury Bill Auction Announcement

Tuesday, March 15, 2011

7:45 A.M.   ICSC Retail Sales Index
8:30 A.M.   Empire State Manufacturing Survey
8:55 A.M.   Johnson Redbook Report
5:00 P.M.   ABC News Consumer Comfort Index

Wednesday, March 16, 2011

7:00 A.M.   U.S. Mortgage Application Indexes

Thursday, March 17, 2011

8:30 A.M.   U.S. Unemployment Insurance Claims
10:00 A.M.   Philadelphia Fed Business Outlook Survey
11:00 A.M.   13- and 26-Week U.S. T-Bill Auction Announcements
4:30 P.M.   U.S. Monetary Aggregates
4:30 P.M.   U.S. Monetary Base

Friday, March 18, 2011

10:00 A.M.   March 2011 options expire

Notes:

Table 3   PCE Breakdown

Total PCE		PCE Ex-Food and Energy, a.k.a. "Core PCE"
Total Index	100%	N/A
Food	13.8	N/A
Energy	6.4	N/A
Core Index	79.8	100%
Shelter	15.0	18.8
Owner's Equivalent Rent (OER)	11.0	13.8
Rent	3.0	3.8
Lodging	0.8	1.0
Medical Services	17.3	21.6
Services ex energy, medical, and shelter	25.0	31.3
Durable Goods	11.0	13.8
Non-Durable Goods ex food and energy	11.6	

The PI figures also include the personal savings rate and personal consumer expenditures (PCE). The PCE index measures changes in prices affecting consumers but it is based on data in the GDP. The PCE extracts from GDP reporting data that shows changes in prices based on items consumers recently purchased. PCE is similar in principle to the Consumer Price Index (CPI), yet based on a different set of metrics. Table 3 shows the breakdown of PCE.

Personal Income is yet another indicator of economic health, and can have a substantial impact on the prices of stocks, bonds, and other securities. Increases in personal income figures may signal an upcoming rise in consumer spending. An actual increase in consumer spending, as registered by PCE, is likely to bring good news to firms selling their products to consumers, as well as these firms' suppliers and auxiliary service providers.

ARE CORPORATE PROFITS A MEANINGFUL ECONOMIC INDICATOR?

Preliminary and final GDP figures, released two and three months (respectively) after each quarter end, are accompanied by a release of Corporate Profits. The Corporate Profits indicator is designed to measure the aggregate corporate activity in the country.

MARCH 21–27, 2011

Events this week:

- U.S. Durable Goods Orders for February 2011
- New Single-Family Home Sales for February 2011
- PCE- and GDP-Based Price Indexes for February 2011

Monday, March 21, 2011

Spring Equinox (Japan Markets Closed)

11:00 A.M.   U.S. Treasury Bill Auction Announcement

Tuesday, March 22, 2011

7:45 A.M.   ICSC Retail Sales Index

8:55 A.M.   Johnson Redbook Report

10:00 A.M.   Richmond Federal Reserve Bank Survey for February 2011

5:00 P.M.   ABC News Consumer Comfort Index

Wednesday, March 23, 2011

7:00 A.M.   U.S. Mortgage Application Indexes

8:00 A.M.   Bank of England Minutes of the Monetary Policy Committee (U.K.)

Thursday, March 24, 2011

8:30 A.M.   U.S. Unemployment Insurance Claims

11:00 A.M.   13- and 26-Week U.S. T-Bill Auction Announcements

4:30 P.M.   U.S. Monetary Aggregates

4:30 P.M.   U.S. Monetary Base

Friday, March 25, 2011

10:00 A.M.   U.S. Consumer Sentiment, final data

10:00 A.M.   Existing Home Sales for February 2011

Notes:

MARCH

The Department of Commerce at the Bureau of Economic Analysis calculates and reports corporate profits in two ways.

- Corporate profits reported in quarterly tax filings.
- Economic corporate profits based on earnings from production in the latest quarter, with various tax deductions added back to reflect true earnings.

Tax-based or "reported" earnings tend to be released first, before economic profits, yet do not tend to move the markets. Tax-based profits are not fully reflective of economic activity: For example, reported earnings for tax purposes would subtract expenses channeled into research and development, depreciation, and similar functions.

The economic corporate profit figures are closer estimates of corporate activity. They are calculated as tax-based corporate profits with discretionary tax adjustments added back to more closely approximate actual corporate earnings. Even such an adjusted measure does not fully reflect the state of the corporate landscape as many corporations tend to smooth out their reported quarterly earnings in an attempt to reduce volatility of their stocks. At the time of their release, the economic corporate profits generate a brief intraday reaction in the U.S. markets: a sudden rise in the

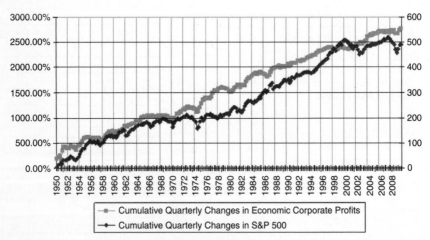

Figure 3   Economic Corporate Profits versus S&P 500.

Events this week:

- Revised GDP Figures, fourth quarter 2010, U.S.
- Revised Personal Income, fourth quarter 2010, U.S.
- Revised Corporate Profits, fourth quarter 2010, U.S.
- Personal Consumption Expenditures for February 2011
- Manufacturers' Shipments, Inventories, and Orders for February 2011
- Construction spending
- U.S. Durable Goods Orders for February 2011
- PCE- and GDP-Based Price Indexes for February 2011

Monday, March 28, 2011

	11:00 A.M.	U.S. Treasury Bill Auction Announcement

Tuesday, March 29, 2011

	7:45 A.M.	ICSC Retail Sales Index
	8:55 A.M.	Johnson Redbook Report
	9:00 A.M.	S&P/Case-Shiller Home Price Indexes for February 2011
	10:00 A.M.	Consumer Confidence
	5:00 P.M.	ABC News Consumer Comfort Index

Wednesday, March 30, 2011

	7:00 A.M.	U.S. Mortgage Application Indexes

Thursday, March 31, 2011

	6:00 A.M.	Monster Employment Index
	8:30 A.M.	U.S. Unemployment Insurance Claims
	9:45 A.M.	Chicago Business Barometer
	10:00 A.M.	Help Wanted Advertising Index for February 2011
	11:00 A.M.	Kansas City Federal Reserve Bank Manufacturing Survey for February 2011
	11:00 A.M.	13- and 26-Week U.S T-Bill Auction Announcements
	4:30 P.M.	U.S. Monetary Aggregates
	4:30 P.M.	U.S. Monetary Base

Notes: _____

U.S. corporate profits is good news for the U.S. economy and is likely to positively affect the U.S. stock markets.

For longer-term investors, however, corporate profits are hardly a useful measure. As Figure 3 (on page 48) shows, quarterly corporate profits are not really correlated with the S&P 500 (contemporaneous correlation between the two variables is 20 percent). While both the S&P 500 and corporate profits rise over time, they do not rise in tandem: In years when corporate profits grow, the S&P 500 may rise or it may fall, and vice versa.

NET EXPORTS AND THE U.S. DOLLAR

Another important component of GDP is Net Exports of good and services. The statistic shows the difference between amounts exported out of the United States and imported into the United States. Net Exports are typically reported as a quarterly percent change.

Net exports document the strength of the U.S. economy and the U.S. dollar relative to other countries. Net exports will rise every quarter when the value of goods exported out of the United States to other countries exceeds the value of goods imported into the United States from abroad. Drivers of foreign demand for U.S. goods may include:

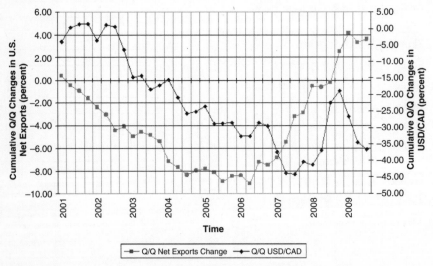

Figure 4   U.S. Net Exports and the U.S./Canada Exchange Rate.

- Advances in U.S. research that are commercialized into new high-quality products, yet unavailable in other countries.

- U.S. productivity improves, enabling the U.S. labor force to produce more products at a lower cost.

- U.S. dollar weakens relative to a foreign currency, reducing the cost of the U.S.-made products in the foreign currency.

The relationship between the strength of currencies and Net Exports turns out to be a two-way street for some countries. Take, for example, Canada. Over 70 percent of Canadian exports are shipped to the United States every year. The demand for the Canadian dollar increases when U.S. firms buy Canadian goods. This strengthens the Canadian dollar, and lowers the U.S./Canada foreign exchange rate. As more Canadian goods are imported into the United States, U.S. Net Exports falls, and the U.S./Canada exchange rate tends to decline. Figure 4 illustrates the relationship between the cumulative quarterly changes in the U.S. Net Exports and the cumulative quarterly changes in U.S./Canadian foreign exchange rate.

SECTORAL PRODUCTION, ORDERS, AND INVENTORIES

2011 APRIL

Sun	Mon	Tue	Wed	Thu	Fri	Sat
					1	2
3	4	5	6	7	8	9
10	11	12	13	14	15	16
17	18	19	20	21	22	23
24	25	26	27	28	29	30

KEY HIGHLIGHTS

To start the second quarter, we examine the announcements on production, orders, and inventories.

- ISM Manufacturing Index Shows Economic Expansions and Contractions
- Regional Fed Surveys: A Tool for Understanding the U.S. Economy
- Durable Goods Orders
- Manufacturers' Shipments, Inventories, and Orders
- Industrial Production and Capacity Utilization

ISM MANUFACTURING INDEX
SHOWS ECONOMIC EXPANSIONS
AND CONTRACTIONS

The Institute for Supply Management (ISM) reports its Manufacturing Index at 10:00 A.M. on the first business day of each month, for the previous month. The Index is a portrait of nearly 350 purchasing agents across different industries. The survey asks whether the purchasing agents expect new orders, production, employment, supplier deliveries, and inventory figures to rise, fall, or remain the same in comparison with the prior month. The Index is assembled as the weighted average of the responses in each category, normalized on a 0–100 scale. Any index value above 50 signifies that more purchasing managers experienced higher growth than lower growth, as compared to the previous month.

The U.S. markets tend to react to the changes in the ISM Manufacturing Index in what appears to be a consistent manner: The markets rise when the Index increases and fall when the Index declines. Figure 5 shows the response of the S&P 500 to a change in the Index. To trade on the ISM Manufacturing

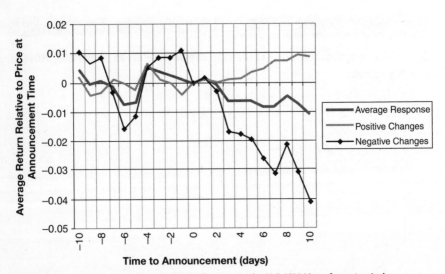

Figure 5   Response of the S&P 500 to Changes in the U.S. ISM Manufacturing Index .

Events this week:

- Manufacturers' Shipments, Inventories, and Orders for February 2011
- Unit Auto and Truck Sales for March 2011
- Challenger, Gray & Christmas Employment Report
- Job Opening and Labor Turnover Survey (JOLTS)

Friday, April 1, 2011

8:30 A.M.	The Employment Situation
10:00 A.M.	Pending Home Sales Index
10:00 A.M.	ISM Report on Business—Manufacturing for March 2011
10:00 A.M.	Construction Spending for February 2011

Notes: _____

Index, a quant investor may choose to buy stocks or ETFs when the Index rises, and sell them when the Index falls.

REGIONAL FED SURVEYS: A TOOL FOR UNDERSTANDING THE U.S. ECONOMY

The U.S. economy is a complex machine with diverse interlocking components. One way to track the state of the economy on aggregate is to follow the monthly reports produced by the Institute for Supply Management (ISM). The ISM reports are divided into the Manufacturing and Non-Manufacturing reports. They are released at 10:00 A.M. on the first and third business day of each month, respectively, and cover the economic conditions of the previous month.

In addition to the ISM survey, six regional surveys regularly report on changes in business conditions. These regional surveys are the Philadelphia Federal Reserve Business Outlook Survey, Empire State Manufacturing Survey, Richmond Federal Reserve Survey, Kansas City Federal Reserve Bank Manufacturing Survey, Texas Manufacturing Outlook Survey, Richmond Federal Reserve Survey of Business Activity, and Chicago Federal Reserve Regional Survey.

The Philadelphia Fed Business Outlook Survey is the oldest of the group, dating back to 1968. It polls manufacturers in the Third Federal Reserve District about their current conditions and their expectations for the future. Specific questions address new and expected orders, delivery times, inventories, prices paid and received, current and projected number of employees, to name a few. The survey participants are asked whether each measure has increased, decreased, or stayed the same, and whether each measure is expected to increase, decrease, or remain stable in the near future. The Philadelphia Fed Survey is released on the third Thursday of every month. Other regional surveys are released from the middle to the end of each month.

The Philadelphia Fed Index was most correlated with prices of key U.S. securities in 2008 and 2009. Table 4 on page 58 shows correlations of changes in the Philadelphia Fed Index with monthly changes in prices of key market securities, such as the S&P 500, crude oil, copper, EUR/USD and

Events this week:

- Unit Auto and Truck Sales for March 2011
- Manufacturers' Shipments, Inventories, and Orders for February 2011
- International Trade Balance for February 2011
- Challenger, Gray & Christmas Employment Report
- Job Opening and Labor Turnover Survey (JOLTS)

Monday, April 4, 2011

11:00 A.M.   U.S. Treasury Bill Auction Announcement

Tuesday, April 5, 2011

7:45 A.M.   ICSC Retail Sales Index

8:55 A.M.   Johnson Redbook Report

10:00 A.M.   ISM Report on Business—Non-Manufacturing for March 2011

5:00 P.M.   ABC News Consumer Comfort Index

Wednesday, April 6, 2011

7:00 A.M.   U.S. Mortgage Application Indexes

8:15 A.M.   ADP National Employment Report

Thursday, April 7, 2011

6:00 A.M.   Monster Employment Index

7:00 A.M.   Bank of England Rate Decision (U.K.)

7:45 A.M.   European Central Bank Interest Rate Announcement

8:30 A.M.   U.S. Unemployment Insurance Claims

11:00 A.M.   13- and 26-Week U.S. T-Bill Auction Announcements

4:30 P.M.   U.S. Monetary Aggregates

4:30 P.M.   U.S. Monetary Base

Friday, April 8, 2011

8:30 A.M.   The Employment Situation

Notes:

Table 4   Correlations of Changes in the Philadelphia Federal Reserve Business Outlook Survey and Key Security Prices, as Measured on Monthly Data for 2008 and 2009

Philadelphia Federal Reserve Business Outlook Survey	Monthly Change in the Price of				
	S&P 500	EUR/USD	USD/JPY	Copper	Crude Oil
Change in the Index value from the previous month	14.3%	-4.9%	14.5%	8.7%	3.7%
Analyst consensus forecast of the Index less last month's realized Index value	47.9%	46.8%	23.2%	29.7%	77.7%

USD/JPY exchange rates. As shown in Table 4, the difference between the consensus forecast and prior realized values of the surveys has the highest correlation with the monthly price changes of crude oil and the S&P 500. This means that a rising consensus forecast often coincides with a rising crude oil price and a rising value for the S&P 500.

The analysts' consensus of expected manufacturing indexes and the Philadelphia Fed Index in particular, can, therefore, be a credible quantitative investment signal.

DURABLE GOODS ORDERS

The Bureau of the Census releases monthly data on orders that have been placed for goods with an expected life of at least three years. Included in these orders are primary metals, electrical and non-electrical machinery, consumer hard goods, transportation equipment (including aircraft and automobiles), and military hardware.

The orders include many categories, some of which are often excluded from event studies. For example, aircraft orders and defense spending are often held apart when reviewing trends in the consumer economy.

The Conference Board's index of leading economic indicators includes these references to durable goods:

- manufacturers' new orders for consumer goods
- manufacturers' new orders for nondefense capital goods

Events this week:

- U.S. NFIB Small Business Optimism Index for March 2011
- Bank of Canada Target Bank Rate Announcement
- U.S. Industrial Production and Capacity Utilization for March 2011
- U.S. Manufacturing and Trade Inventories and Sales for February 2011
- U.S. Retail Sales for March 2011
- Housing Starts and Building Permits for March 2011
- International Trade Balance for February 2011
- Treasury International Capital Flows for February 2011
- Consumer Price Index
- Producer Price Index
- Productivity and Costs
- Import and Export Prices

Monday, April 11, 2011

11:00 A.M.	U.S. Treasury Bill Auction Announcement

Tuesday, April 12, 2011

7:45 A.M.	ICSC Retail Sales Index
8:55 A.M.	Johnson Redbook Report
2:00 P.M.	U.S. Federal Budget Balance
5:00 P.M.	ABC News Consumer Comfort Index

Wednesday, April 13, 2011

7:00 A.M.	U.S. Mortgage Application Indexes
2:00 P.M.	Current Economic Conditions ("Beige Book")

Thursday, April 14, 2011

8:30 A.M.	U.S. Unemployment Insurance Claims
11:00 A.M.	13- and 26-Week U.S. T-Bill Auction Announcements
4:30 P.M.	U.S. Monetary Aggregates
4:30 P.M.	U.S. Monetary Base

Friday, April 15, 2011

8:30 A.M.	Empire State Manufacturing Survey
10:00 A.M.	U.S. Consumer Sentiment, preliminary data
12:00 P.M.	April 2011 options expire

Notes: _____

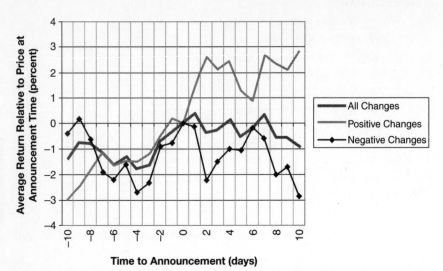

Figure 6　Response of HD to Changes in the U.S. Durable Goods Orders.

Increases in new durable goods orders are often well received by the markets. Figure 6 shows the average response of Home Depot's stock (ticker: HD) to changes in durable goods orders. Home Depot is one of the firms particularly sensitive to changes in durable goods orders since it's a retailer of home appliances, and an increase in manufacturers' orders is a good sign for HD. Increases in orders tend to lift HD, while order decreases often depress HD. To invest in HD upon announcements of changes in durable goods orders, buy HD after an increase in durable goods orders and hold the position for a few days.

MANUFACTURERS' SHIPMENTS, INVENTORIES, AND ORDERS

Each month, the U.S. Department of Commerce compiles and releases statistics on durable and nondurable goods orders, shipments and inventories. Increases in factory orders often signify an improvement in economic conditions, which in turn buoys equity prices, as shown in Figure 7 on page 62 with the share price of Allstate Insurance (ticker: ALL).

Events this week:

- Bank of Canada Target Bank Rate Announcement
- U.S. Durable Goods Orders for March 2011
- Composite Index of Leading Economic Indicators for March 2011
- Housing Starts and Building Permits for March 2011

Monday, April 18, 2011

11:00 A.M.   U.S. Treasury Bill Auction Announcement

Tuesday, April 19, 2011

7:45 A.M.   ICSC Retail Sales Index

8:55 A.M.   Johnson Redbook Report

5:00 P.M.   ABC News Consumer Comfort Index

Wednesday, April 20, 2011

7:00 A.M.   U.S. Mortgage Application Indexes

7:00 A.M.   Bank of England Minutes of the Monetary Policy Committee (U.K.)

Thursday, April 21, 2011

8:30 A.M.   U.S. Unemployment Insurance Claims

10:00 A.M.   Philadelphia Fed Business Outlook Survey

11:00 A.M.   13- and 26-Week U.S. T-Bill Auction Announcements

4:30 P.M.   U.S. Monetary Aggregates

4:30 P.M.   U.S. Monetary Base

Friday, April 22, 2011

Good Friday (U.S. Markets Closed)

Notes:

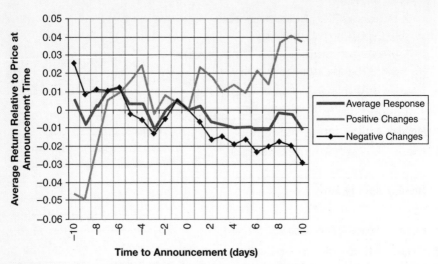

Figure 7   Response of ALL to Changes in the U.S. Factory Orders.

The monthly release on factory orders is at 10:00 A.M. four to five weeks after the end of the month for which the data is reported. To profitably trade on factory orders, buy (sell) ALL after an announcement of positive (negative) change in factory orders, and update your position after the following factory orders news release. We cannot guarantee that ALL will move in conjunction with factory orders but Figure 3 shows a trend.

A recent survey of 37 state insurance-fraud bureaus by the Coalition Against Insurance Fraud found that the recession "appears to have had a significant impact on the incidence of fraud." The survey found that questionable claims were up 14 percent from 2008.

Durable goods orders account for about 52 percent of factory orders reported. Separate monthly data on durable goods orders is typically released one week prior to the announcement of factory orders. As a result, some information contained in factory orders figures is already incorporated into market prices before release of factory orders data. Stocks of durable goods manufacturers tend not to respond to factory orders announcements in a consistent manner.

Events this week:

- Advance GDP Figures, first quarter 2011, U.S.
- Advance Personal Income, first quarter 2010, U.S.
- Manufacturers' Shipments, Inventories, and Orders for March 2011
- Personal Consumption Expenditures for March 2011
- U.S. Durable Goods Orders for March 2011
- Housing Vacancies and Homeownership Rates
- PCE- and GDP-Based Price Indexes for March 2011
- Employment Cost Index for first quarter 2011

APR/MAY

Monday, April 25, 2011

Easter Monday (U.K. Markets Closed)

🏠	10:00 A.M.	Existing Home Sales for March 2011
💰	11:00 A.M.	U.S. Treasury Bill Auction Announcement

Tuesday, April 26, 2011

🛒	7:45 A.M.	ICSC Retail Sales Index
🛒	8:55 A.M.	Johnson Redbook Report
🏠	9:00 A.M.	S&P/Case-Shiller Home Price Indexes for March 2011
🌐	10:00 A.M.	Richmond Federal Reserve Bank Survey for March 2011
🛒	10:00 A.M.	Consumer Confidence
🛒	5:00 P.M.	ABC News Consumer Comfort Index

Wednesday, April 27, 2011

🏠	7:00 A.M.	U.S. Mortgage Application Indexes

Thursday, April 28, 2011

💼	8:30 A.M.	U.S. Unemployment Insurance Claims
💼	10:00 A.M.	Help Wanted Advertising Index for March 2011
🌐	11:00 A.M.	Kansas City Federal Reserve Bank Manufacturing Survey for March 2011
💰	11:00 A.M.	13- and 26-Week U.S. T-Bill Auction Announcements
📈	4:30 P.M.	U.S. Monetary Aggregates
📈	4:30 P.M.	U.S. Monetary Base

Friday, April 29, 2011

Showa Day (Japan Markets Closed)

🌐	9:45 A.M.	Chicago Business Barometer
🛒	10:00 A.M.	U.S. Consumer Sentiment, final data

Notes: _____
_____
_____
_____
_____
_____
_____
_____
_____
_____
_____
_____
_____
_____
_____
_____
_____
_____
_____
_____
_____
_____
_____
_____
_____
_____
_____
_____
_____
_____
_____

INDUSTRIAL PRODUCTION AND CAPACITY UTILIZATION

The Federal Reserve distributes a monthly report on the output and utilization of manufacturing firms, mines, and utilities.

Manufacturing is the largest of the three sectors, representing about 80 percent of the groups' total output. Mines and utilities represent about 10 percent each. Manufacturing includes:

- Chemicals (about 12%)
- Food and tobacco products (11%)
- Computer and electronic products (8%)
- Printing and publishing (7%)
- Fabricated metals (6%)
- Motor vehicles and parts (5%)
- Machinery (5%)

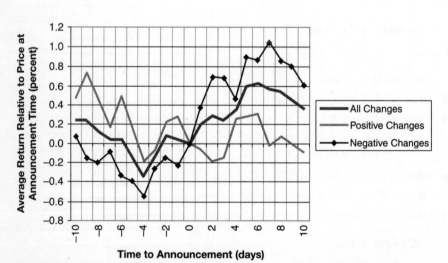

Figure 8   Response of Euro/U.S. Dollar Exchange Rate to Changes in the U.S. Industrial Production.

The capacity utilization report provides insights into the amount of flexibility in the economy. When combined with announcements about inventory, a picture of the state of the economy's supply chain emerges.

During a recovery from a recession, monitoring the state of the country's inventory creates an impression about whether demand is rebounding or whether the supply chain remains slack. This can also have repercussions for inflation expectations.

Higher industrial production in the United States is greeted as a sign of a strengthening economy and a strengthening U.S. dollar. Figure 8 shows the average response of the Euro/U.S. dollar exchange rate following announced changes in U.S. industrial production. Following positive changes in industrial production, the Euro declines relative to the U.S. dollar (U.S. dollar strengthens). Conversely, the Euro rises relative to the U.S. dollar (U.S. dollar weakens) if industrial production declines.

APR/MAY

CONSUMER SPENDING AND CONFIDENCE

2011 MAY

Sun	Mon	Tue	Wed	Thu	Fri	Sat
1	2	3	4	5	6	7
8	9	10	11	12	13	14
15	16	17	18	19	20	21
22	23	24	25	26	27	28
29	30	31				

KEY HIGHLIGHTS

The focus of May is on the consumer. This month we discuss indicators of consumer spending and overall confidence in the economy.

- Retail Sales Index Has a Short-Term Impact on U.S. Stocks
- Johnson Redbook Report
- Consumer Confidence Buoys the Markets
- ABC News Consumer Comfort Index
- U.S. Consumer Sentiment

RETAIL SALES INDEX HAS A
SHORT-TERM IMPACT ON U.S. STOCKS

Numerous surveys have been developed over the years to help investors gain insight into the spending behavior of an average consumer. As spending patterns drive growth in many parts of the economy, these surveys help quant investors anticipate upcoming corporate earnings announcements and the state of the economy as a whole.

To review whether the consumer's wallet is thick and open to spending, the Bureau of the Census at the U.S. Department of Commerce aggregates dollar amounts individuals spend through various channels, including retailers, new and used auto dealerships, and food stores. The data is compiled monthly and is adjusted for seasonal variations.

Increases in retail sales typically signify good news. Higher consumer purchases stimulate the economy, and the U.S. stock markets tend to respond positively to rising retail sales figures. For example, Figure 9 shows response of IBM stock to announced changes in retail sales. IBM retails computers and other technology, in addition to distributing products wholesale.

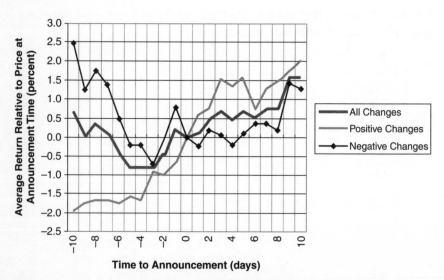

Figure 9   Response of IBM to Changes in the U.S Retail Sales.

Events this week:

- Pending Home Sales Index
- Challenger, Gray & Christmas Employment Report
- Unit Auto and Truck Sales for April 2011
- ISM Semiannual Report
- Manufacturers' Shipments, Inventories, and Orders for March 2011
- Job Opening and Labor Turnover Survey (JOLTS)

Monday, May 2, 2011

May Day (U.K. Markets Closed)

	10:00 A.M.	ISM Report on Business—Manufacturing for April 2011
	10:00 A.M.	Construction Spending for March 2011
	11:00 A.M.	U.S. Treasury Bill Auction Announcement

Tuesday, May 3, 2011

Constitutional Day (Japan Markets Closed)

	7:45 A.M.	ICSC Retail Sales Index
	8:55 A.M.	Johnson Redbook Report
	5:00 P.M.	ABC News Consumer Comfort Index

Wednesday, May 4, 2011

Greenery Day (Japan Markets Closed)

	7:00 A.M.	U.S. Mortgage Application Indexes
	8:15 A.M.	ADP National Employment Report
	10:00 A.M.	ISM Report on Business—Non-Manufacturing for April 2011

Thursday, May 5, 2011

Children's Day (Japan Markets Closed)

	6:00 A.M.	Monster Employment Index
	7:00 A.M.	Bank of England Rate Decision (U.K.)
	7:45 A.M.	European Central Bank Interest Rate Announcement
	8:30 A.M.	U.S. Unemployment Insurance Claims
	10:00 A.M.	OFHEO Home Price Index, U.S.
	11:00 A.M.	13- and 26-Week U.S. T-Bill Auction Announcements
	4:30 P.M.	U.S. Monetary Aggregates
	4:30 P.M.	U.S. Monetary Base

Friday, May 6, 2011

	8:30 A.M.	The Employment Situation

Notes: _____

MAY

The impact of retail sales news tends to be short-lived, however. As illustrated in Figure 9 on page 68, if the latest change in U.S. retail sales is positive, the impact of the news on IBM's stock lasts for three days, on average. If the latest news is negative, the impact on IBM is just one day.

JOHNSON REDBOOK REPORT

For frequent investment signals related to the spending patterns of consumers, consider the Johnson Redbook Report. This is a weekly indicator, often used to refine the information generated by more comprehensive sources that may only report monthly or quarterly.

The Redbook index measures changes in the sales of department stores for the previous week. Redbook figures are reported every Tuesday at 8:55 A.M. The index is based on sales information of 12 major department stores with nearly 9,000 stores nationwide.

Positive changes in the Redbook index indicate a stronger U.S. dollar and more robust economy, from a consumer standpoint. Figure 10 illustrates how the currency markets react to Redbook announcements. Following an increase in the Redbook index, the Euro drops relative to the U.S. dollar (U.S. dollar strengthens), and vice versa.

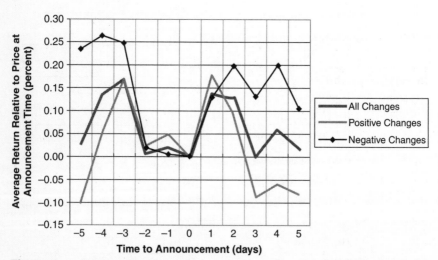

Figure 10   Response of Euro/U.S. Dollar Exchange Rate to Changes in the U.S. Redbook Index.

MAY 9–15, 2011

Events this week:

- U.S. NFIB Small Business Optimism Index for April 2011
- U.S. Industrial Production and Capacity Utilization for April 2011
- U.S. Retail Sales for April 2011
- U.S. Manufacturing and Trade Inventories and Sales for March 2011
- ISM Semiannual Report
- International Trade Balance for March 2011
- Treasury International Capital Flows for March 2011
- Job Opening and Labor Turnover Survey (JOLTS)
- Consumer Price Index
- Producer Price Index
- Productivity and Costs
- Import and Export Prices

MAY

Monday, May 9, 2011

| 11:00 A.M. | U.S. Treasury Bill Auction Announcement |

Tuesday, May 10, 2011

7:45 A.M.	ICSC Retail Sales Index
8:55 A.M.	Johnson Redbook Report
5:00 P.M.	ABC News Consumer Comfort Index

Wednesday, May 11, 2011

7:00 A.M.	U.S. Mortgage Application Indexes
7:00 A.M.	Bank of England Inflation Report (U.K.)
2:00 P.M.	U.S. Federal Budget Balance

Thursday, May 12, 2011

8:30 A.M.	U.S. Unemployment Insurance Claims
11:00 A.M.	13- and 26-Week U.S. T-Bill Auction Announcements
4:30 P.M.	U.S. Monetary Aggregates
4:30 P.M.	U.S. Monetary Base

Friday, May 13, 2011

| 10:00 A.M. | U.S. Consumer Sentiment, preliminary data |

Notes:

CONSUMER CONFIDENCE BUOYS
THE MARKETS

Whereas sales figures document actual spending from the past, consumer confidence measures are leading indicators of the direction of the economy according to survey respondents.

One such survey is the Taylor Nelson Sofres survey. It is a national survey of 5,000 households performed every month to assess their views on a variety of topics that include the economy, their careers, likelihood of buying a house, buying durable goods, and going on vacations. Not surprisingly, higher consumer confidence in the United States tends to lift the U.S. stock markets.

Figure 11 shows the average responses of the iShares Dow Jones U.S. Home Construction ETF (ticker: ITB) to changes in consumer confidence. As the consumer feels more confident, the shares of ITB climb higher. Unlike consumer sentiment announcements, where the equity prices tend to uniformly decline on the day immediately following the announcement day, consumer confidence announcements trigger a clear-cut positive response in equities to rises in confidence and a negative response to setbacks.

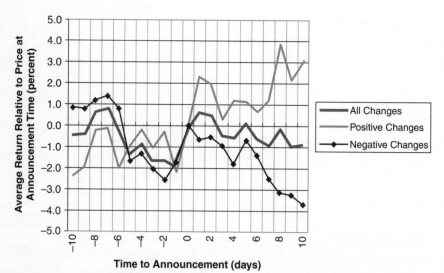

Figure 11   Response of ITB to Changes in the U.S. Consumer Confidence Index.

Events this week:

- U.S. Durable Goods Orders for April 2011
- Composite Index of Leading Economic Indicators for April 2011
- Housing Starts and Building Permits for April 2011
- Treasury International Capital Flows for March 2011
- Consumer Price Index

Monday, May 16, 2011

	8:30 A.M.	Empire State Manufacturing Survey
	11:00 A.M.	U.S. Treasury Bill Auction Announcement

Notes: _____

Tuesday, May 17, 2011

	7:45 A.M.	ICSC Retail Sales Index
	8:55 A.M.	Johnson Redbook Report
	5:00 P.M.	ABC News Consumer Comfort Index

Wednesday, May 18, 2011

	7:00 A.M.	U.S. Mortgage Application Indexes
	7:00 A.M.	Bank of England Minutes of the Monetary Policy Committee (U.K.)

Thursday, May 19, 2011

	8:30 A.M.	U.S. Unemployment Insurance Claims
	10:00 A.M.	Philadelphia Fed Business Outlook Survey
	11:00 A.M.	13- and 26-Week U.S. T-Bill Auction Announcements
	4:30 P.M.	U.S. Monetary Aggregates
	4:30 P.M.	U.S. Monetary Base

Friday, May 20, 2011

	12:00 P.M.	May 2011 options expire

MAY

ABC NEWS CONSUMER COMFORT INDEX

ABC News has developed its own proprietary index in order to profile the economic behavior of American consumers. The ABC News Consumer Comfort Index provides a weekly perspective on how consumers feel about a range of topics that affect their personal finances.

This index is released every Tuesday at 5 P.M. and has gauged consumer sentiment since 1985.

According to the ABC polling group, "Interviews for the ABC News Consumer Comfort Index" are reported as a four-week rolling average. The results are based on telephone interviews among a random national sample of 1,000 adults. The results have a three-point error margin.

Whereas the ICSC Retail Sales Index tracks sales at a selection of stores, the ABC Index is a poll of individuals and how they feel about the strength of the economy and their finances. The poll covers attitudes about consumers' personal finances and their views on the state of the economy. The survey is useful in that it breaks down its statistics in a variety of groupings, including by demographic, political party, and regional affiliation.

Higher Consumer Comfort Index values are likely to have a positive impact on the U.S. equity markets. In recessions, the Consumer Comfort Index falls sharply, as Figure 12 shows.

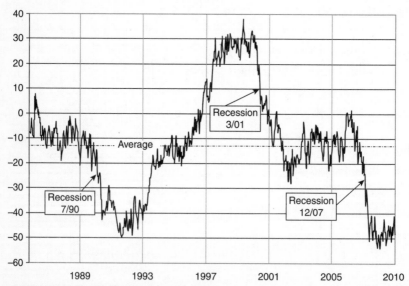

Figure 12   ABC News Consumer Comfort Index.

Note: Weekly tracking results since December 1985.

Events this week:

- U.S. Durable Goods Orders for April 2011
- Bank of Canada Target Bank Rate Announcement
- Manufacturers' Shipments, Inventories, and Orders for April 2011
- Personal Consumption Expenditures for April 2011
- PCE- and GDP-Based Price Indexes for April 2011

Monday, May 23, 2011

Queen Victoria's Birthday (Canadian Markets Closed)

11:00 A.M.   U.S. Treasury Bill Auction Announcement

Tuesday, May 24, 2011

7:45 A.M.   ICSC Retail Sales Index

8:55 A.M.   Johnson Redbook Report

10:00 A.M.   Richmond Federal Reserve Bank Survey for April 2011

5:00 P.M.   ABC News Consumer Comfort Index

Wednesday, May 25, 2011

7:00 A.M.   U.S. Mortgage Application Indexes

10:00 A.M.   Existing Home Sales for April 2011

Thursday, May 26, 2011

8:30 A.M.   U.S. Unemployment Insurance Claims

10:00 A.M.   ISM Report on Non-Manufacturing sectors

10:00 A.M.   Help Wanted Advertising Index for April 2011

11:00 A.M.   Kansas City Federal Reserve Bank Manufacturing
Survey for April 2011

11:00 A.M.   13- and 26-Week U.S. T-Bill Auction Announcements

4:30 P.M.   U.S. Monetary Aggregates

4:30 P.M.   U.S. Monetary Base

Friday, May 27, 2011

10:00 A.M.   U.S. Consumer Sentiment, final data

8:30 A.M.   The Employment Situation

Notes: _____

MAY

U.S. CONSUMER SENTIMENT

A variety of surveys measure consumer confidence. Each survey has a different focus with an objective to highlight distinct features of economic growth.

The U.S. Consumer Sentiment Index tries to do it all. Collected and released semi-monthly by Reuters and University of Michigan, the Index is an aggregate of the current and expected future economic conditions of 500 American men and women polled by the index team. The one- and five-year expectations formed by the poll are included in the U.S. leading indicators, reported separately.

Figure 13 shows the response of iShares Dow Jones U.S. Home Construction ETF (ticker: ITB) to changes in consumer sentiment. As the U.S. consumers' optimism rises, so do the ITB shares. Interestingly, ITB on average falls on the day immediately following a positive change consumer sentiment announcement, then rises steadily to capture 3 percent over the following week.

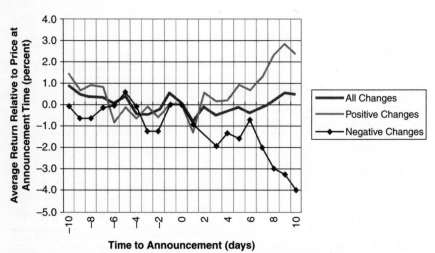

Figure 13   Response of ITB to Changes in the U.S. Consumer Sentiment.

Events this week:

- Preliminary GDP Figures, first quarter 2011, U.S.
- Preliminary Personal Income, first quarter 2011, U.S.
- Preliminary Corporate Profits, first quarter 2011, U.S.
- Pending Home Sales Index
- Challenger, Gray & Christmas Employment Report
- Bank of Canada Target Bank Rate Announcement
- Manufacturers' Shipments, Inventories, and Orders for April 2011
- PCE- and GDP-Based Price Indexes for April 2011

Monday, May 30, 2011

U.S. Memorial Day (U.S. Markets Closed)
U.K. Summer Bank Holiday (U.K. Markets Closed)

Notes:

Tuesday, May 31, 2011

7:45 A.M.   ICSC Retail Sales Index
8:55 A.M.   Johnson Redbook Report
9:00 A.M.   S&P/Case-Shiller Home Price Indexes for April 2011
9:45 A.M.   Chicago Business Barometer
10:00 A.M.   Consumer Confidence
5:00 P.M.   ABC News Consumer Comfort Index

MAY/JUNE

HOUSING AND CONSTRUCTION

2011 JUNE

Sun	Mon	Tue	Wed	Thu	Fri	Sat
		1	2	3	4	
5	6	7	8	9	10	11
12	13	14	15	16	17	18
19	20	21	22	23	24	25
26	27	28	29	30		

JUNE

KEY HIGHLIGHTS

Typically, summer is the busiest season for buying and moving into a new home. As such, housing and construction is the topic for June.

- Construction Spending Is Good News to Some
- Falling Numbers of Prospective Homebuyers Is Bad News for Equity Markets in the United States
- New Single-Family Home Sales Drive Markets
- S&P/Case-Shiller Home Price Index
- Need Additional Precision in Housing Data? Try These Indicators

CONSTRUCTION SPENDING IS GOOD
NEWS TO SOME

Construction spending on public projects like highways or on private projects drives substantial amounts of capital into the economy. Whether the project is public, residential, commercial, or industrial, announcements of new construction tend to be a quantitative indicator of the health of the economy.

The data released on construction spending is often used to make inferences about a variety of sectors serving as inputs to construction, such as forestry and mining. The construction announcements can also be statistically valid, yet not have intuitive relationships with stocks, such as the relationship with the stock of the Allstate Insurance, shown in the figure below.

Figure 14 shows the response of shares of Allstate Insurance (ticker: ALL) to positive and negative construction spending announcements. Growth in construction spending is coincident with a clear rise in ALL stock, at least in the near term. As several housing-related figures are reported ahead of construction spending, ALL stock begins to incorporate the positive economic news a few days before construction spending is announced. Yet, quantitative investor can successfully trade on the construction spending announcements

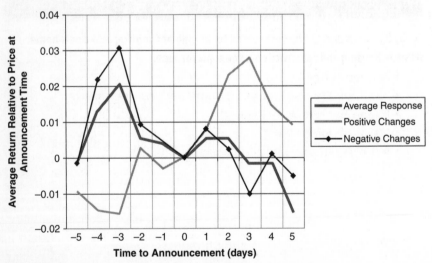

Figure 14   Response of S&P 500 to Changes in the U.S. MBA Purchase Applications.

MAY 30–JUNE 5, 2011

Events this week:

- Manufacturers' Shipments, Inventories, and Orders for May 2011
- Unit Auto and Truck Sales for May 2011
- Pending Home Sales, U.S.
- Challenger, Gray & Christmas Employment Report
- Job Opening and Labor Turnover Survey (JOLTS)

Wednesday, June 1, 2011

🏠	7:00 A.M.	U.S. Mortgage Application Indexes
💼	8:15 A.M.	ADP National Employment Report
⚙	10:00 A.M.	ISM Report on Business—Manufacturing for May 2011
🏠	10:00 A.M.	Construction Spending for April 2011

Thursday, June 2, 2011

💼	6:00 A.M.	Monster Employment Index
💼	8:30 A.M.	U.S. Unemployment Insurance Claims
📈	4:30 P.M.	U.S. Monetary Aggregates
📈	4:30 P.M.	U.S. Monetary Base

Friday, June 3, 2011

💼	8:30 A.M.	The Employment Situation
⚙	10:00 A.M.	ISM Report on Business—Non-Manufacturing for May 2011

Notes:

as follows: Buy (sell) ALL stock immediately following a positive (negative) construction spending figure and reverse the position in three days. One explanation for the observed relationship between construction spending and the stock of Allstate Insurance may lie in the expectation of increased insurance business following higher construction figures.

FALLING NUMBERS OF PROSPECTIVE HOMEBUYERS IS BAD NEWS FOR EQUITY MARKETS IN THE UNITED STATES

People tend to buy homes when times are good. Not surprisingly, the number of prospective homebuyers sends a direct signal to the market. When the number of prospective homebuyers rises in comparison with the prior week, so does the S&P 500, at least temporarily, as Figure 15 shows. When the number falls, the S&P 500 declines as well.

The number of prospective homebuyers in the United States is available as an index, compiled weekly by the Mortgage Bankers Association (MBA). Every week, the MBA tallies the number of mortgage loan applications received by the banks that are members of the MBA. The numbers, aggregated into relative indexes, are then reported on Wednesdays, at 7:00 A.M. Eastern Time. On July 8, 2009, for example, the Purchase Index Level

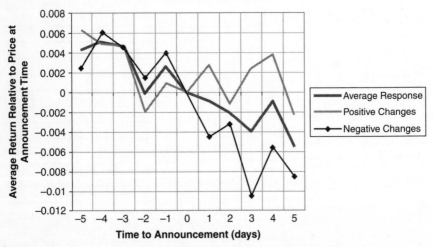

Figure 15   Response of ALL to Changes in the U.S. Construction Spending.

Events this week:

- International Trade Balance for April 2011
- Job Opening and Labor Turnover Survey (JOLTS)
- Productivity and Costs
- Import and Export Prices
- Flow of Funds

Monday, June 6, 2011

11:00 A.M.   U.S. Treasury Bill Auction Announcement

Tuesday, June 7, 2011

7:45 A.M.   ICSC Retail Sales Index

8:55 A.M.   Johnson Redbook Report

5:00 P.M.   ABC News Consumer Comfort Index

Wednesday, June 8, 2011

7:00 A.M.   U.S. Mortgage Application Indexes

2:00 P.M.   Current Economic Conditions ("Beige Book")

Thursday, June 9, 2011

7:00 A.M.   Bank of England Rate Decision

7:45 A.M.   European Central Bank Interest Rate Announcement

8:30 A.M.   U.S. Unemployment Insurance Claims

11:00 A.M.   13- and 26-Week U.S. T-Bill Auction Announcements

4:30 P.M.   U.S. Monetary Aggregates

4:30 P.M.   U.S. Monetary Base

Friday, June 10, 2011

10:00 A.M.   U.S. Consumer Sentiment, preliminary data

2:00 P.M.   U.S. Federal Budget Balance

Notes:

JUNE

was reported as 285.6, up from 267.7 a week earlier. While the index levels do not directly translate into the number of mortgage applications received by banks that week, the relative change in the index provides a meaningful quantitative assessment of the direction, magnitude, and trend in mortgage applications.

The MBA produces several indexes: residential mortgage applications, refinancing applications, index of all mortgage applications, as well as indexes of mortgages broken down by their type: conventional or government insured, fixed-rate or adjustable. The impact of each of these can be analyzed quantitatively to obtain a more textured picture of upcoming market responses in the wake of each announcement.

NEW SINGLE-FAMILY HOME SALES DRIVE MARKETS

Sales volumes and prices of new single-family homes are reported by the Department of Commerce on a monthly basis. This report identifies the homes actually sold in the previous month as measured by a signed contract or deposit.

This report dates back to 1963 and it is adjusted for seasonality.

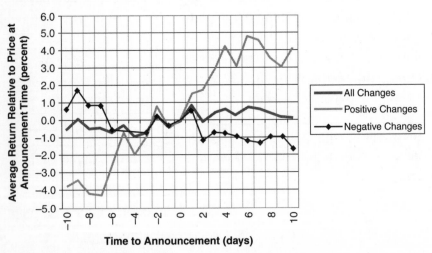

Figure 16   Response of HD to Changes in the U.S. New Home Sales.

Events this week:

- U.S. NFIB Small Business Optimism Index for May 2011
- U.S. Industrial Production and Capacity Utilization for May 2011
- U.S. Manufacturing and Trade Inventories and Sales for April 2011
- U.S. Retail Sales for May 2011
- Composite Index of Leading Economic Indicators for May 2011
- Housing Starts and Building Permits for May 2011
- International Trade Balance for April 2011
- Current Account Balance, first quarter 2011
- Treasury International Capital Flows for April 2011
- Consumer Price Index
- Producer Price Index
- Productivity and Costs
- Import and Export Prices
- Flow of Funds

Monday, June 13, 2011

11:00 A.M.   U.S. Treasury Bill Auction Announcement

Tuesday, June 14, 2011

12:01 A.M.   Manpower Employment Outlook Survey

7:45 A.M.   ICSC Retail Sales Index

8:55 A.M.   Johnson Redbook Report

5:00 P.M.   ABC News Consumer Comfort Index

Wednesday, June 15, 2011

7:00 A.M.   U.S. Mortgage Application Indexes

8:30 A.M.   Empire State Manufacturing Survey

Thursday, June 16, 2011

8:30 A.M.   U.S. Unemployment Insurance Claims

10:00 A.M.   Philadelphia Fed Business Outlook Survey

11:00 A.M.   13- and 26-Week U.S. T-Bill Auction Announcements

4:30 P.M.   U.S. Monetary Aggregates

4:30 P.M.   U.S. Monetary Base

Friday, June 17, 2011

12:00 P.M.   June 2011 options expire

Notes:

One of the notable features of the New Home Sales report is that only homes where the land and building are sold together are included in the data. Homes that are built on land previously purchased by the owner are treated separately. The Department of Commerce also tracks the inventory of new homes for sale and monitors the inventory levels of new homes.

Once again, let's examine the response of Home Depot (ticker: HD) stock to changes in new home sales. Home Depot is a retailer of home renovation products and appliances, and an increase in new home owners often means additional business for HD. As Figure 16 (on page 84) shows, the HD stock responds as projected: HD rises following increases in new home sales and falls when new home sales drop.

S&P/CASE-SHILLER HOME PRICE INDEX

The S&P/Case-Shiller Home Price Index tracks changes in the value of the residential real estate market in 20 metropolitan regions across the United States. The index is issued on a monthly basis for the 20 regions and quarterly nation-wide.

This index is a key measure of the stability of the housing sector.

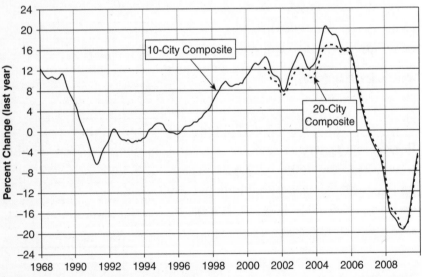

Figure 17   S&P/Case-Shiller Home Price Index.

Source: Standard & Poor's and Fisery.

JUNE 20–26, 2011

Events this week:

- Existing Home Sales for May 2011
- U.S. Durable Goods Orders for May 2011

Monday, June 20, 2011

💵	11:00 A.M.	U.S. Treasury Bill Auction Announcement

Tuesday, June 21, 2011

🛒	7:45 A.M.	ICSC Retail Sales Index
🛒	8:55 A.M.	Johnson Redbook Report
🛒	5:00 P.M.	ABC News Consumer Comfort Index

Wednesday, June 22, 2011

🏠	7:00 A.M.	U.S. Mortgage Application Indexes
💵	7:00 A.M.	Bank of England Minutes of the Monetary Policy Committee (U.K)

Thursday, June 23, 2011

💼	8:30 A.M.	U.S. Unemployment Insurance Claims
💵	11:00 A.M.	13- and 26-Week U.S. T-Bill Auction Announcements
📈	4:30 P.M.	U.S. Monetary Aggregates
📈	4:30 P.M.	U.S. Monetary Base

Friday, June 24, 2011

🛒	10:00 P.M.	U.S. Consumer Sentiment, preliminary data

Notes: _____

JUNE

The Index is based on the sale of existing single-family homes. It includes typical arms-length deals but not the transactions among family members or real estate developers. The information comes from county assessors and recorders.

The index indicates the health of the real estate markets and impacts the equity values in related industries, such as construction (see Figure 17 on page 86).

NEED ADDITIONAL PRECISION IN
HOUSING DATA? TRY THESE INDICATORS

To account for different facets of housing sales, a cottage industry of additional housing market indexes has sprung up in the United States. Various private and public associations involved with building, renovating, and selling houses publish their own statistics, each trying to spotlight a unique aspect of the market. Together, these indexes contribute to the mosaic of the housing situation in the country.

The following indexes are available to investors seeking the latest updates on U.S. housing.

- Housing Market Index
- Mortgage Delinquencies and Foreclosures
- Housing Vacancies and Homeownership Rates
- Housing Starts and Building Permits

The Housing Market Index (HMI) is prepared by the National Association of Home Builders (NAHB). Every month, the NAHB asks its members to assess current sales and near-term sales expectations for single-family housing. Rising sales and home builder optimism about the future serve as a positive signal for U.S. equity markets.

The quarterly index of residential delinquencies and foreclosures is released by the Mortgage Banker Association. Increases in delinquencies indicate bad news for banks as well as for other sectors of the U.S. economy.

The Bureau of the Census at the U.S. Department of Commerce reports the changes in the home vacancy indexes, as well as homeowner occupancy rates. The rental vacancy rate measures the percentage of all available rental

Events this week:

- Revised GDP Figures, first quarter 2011, U.S.
- Revised Personal Income, first quarter 2011, U.S.
- Revised Corporate Profits, first quarter 2011, U.S.
- Manufacturers' Shipments, Inventories, and Orders for May 2011
- Personal Consumption Expenditures for May 2011
- U.S. Durable Goods Orders for May 2011
- Existing Home Sales for May 2011
- PCE- and GDP-Based Price Indexes for May 2011

Monday, June 27, 2011

	11:00 A.M.	U.S. Treasury Bill Auction Announcement

Tuesday, June 28, 2011

	7:45 A.M.	ICSC Retail Sales Index
	8:55 A.M.	Johnson Redbook Report
	9:00 A.M.	S&P/Case-Shiller Home Price Indexes for May 2011
	10:00 A.M.	Richmond Federal Reserve Bank Survey for May 2011
	10:00 A.M.	Consumer Confidence
	5:00 P.M.	ABC News Consumer Comfort Index

Wednesday, June 29, 2011

	7:00 A.M.	U.S. Mortgage Application Indexes

Thursday, June 30, 2011

	8:30 A.M.	U.S. Unemployment Insurance Claims
	9:45 A.M.	Chicago Business Barometer
	10:00 A.M.	Help Wanted Advertising Index for May 2011
	11:00 A.M.	Kansas City Federal Reserve Bank Manufacturing Survey for May 2011
	11:00 A.M.	13- and 26-Week U.S. T-Bill Auction Announcements
	4:30 P.M.	U.S. Monetary Aggregates
	4:30 P.M.	U.S. Monetary Base

Notes: _____

_____

_____

_____

_____

_____

_____

_____

_____

_____

_____

_____

_____

_____

_____

_____

_____

_____

_____

_____

_____

_____

_____

_____

_____

_____

_____

_____

JUNE/JULY

units that are vacant. The homeowner vacancy rate assesses the number of units that are vacant and for sale. The homeownership rate is the percentage of occupied housing units that are owner-occupied. Higher vacancies may indicate oversupply of housing units, while higher owner occupancy is good news for banks—many consumers are likely to pay their home mortgage.

The monthly summary of the building activity of new private homes is compiled by the Department of Commerce releases. These are signaled by the flow of requests for permits. While not all towns and villages require permits, this report provides insights going back to 1959 about the percentage changes in residential building activity.

Other indexes measuring the state of housing include the Existing Home Sales, Pending Home Sales, and Affordability Indexes released by the National Association of Realtors, and the OFHEO Home Price Index based on consecutive sales of the same house as recorded by loans purchased or securitized by Fannie Mae or Freddie Mac.

FOREIGN TRADE AND INTERNATIONAL CAPITAL FLOW

2011 JULY

Sun	Mon	Tue	Wed	Thu	Fri	Sat
					1	2
3	4	5	6	7	8	9
10	11	12	13	14	15	16
17	18	19	20	21	22	23
24	25	26	27	28	29	30
31						

JULY

KEY HIGHLIGHTS

With growing globalization, foreign trade and international capital flows have an increasingly tangible impact on domestic markets in many countries worldwide. Here, we examine the associated issues.

- Looking to Invest Long-Term? Check Current Account Balance for Economic Trends
- Current Account Balance and the U.S. Dollar
- Higher International Trade = Lower U.S. Stocks
- TICS and Foreign Exchange Investing
- Foreign Flows into U.S. Bonds Lower U.S. Interest Rates

91

LOOKING TO INVEST LONG-TERM? CHECK CURRENT ACCOUNT BALANCE FOR ECONOMIC TRENDS

The Current Account Balance measures the country's international inflows and outflows of capital and therefore reflects the domestics economic situation. As a result, the Current Account Balance has been shown to have a relationship with the country's business cycle. In particular, Caroline Freund of the Federal Reserve (*Journal of International Money and Finance*, 2005) found that the Current Account is counter-cyclical relative to the current business cycle. The current account worsens when economic growth is above its trend line, and it improves when a country is in recession.

Naturally, quant investors use the quarterly changes in the current account to identify long-term trends in economic growth. Figure 18 illustrates the premise on Net Current Account Balance of the United States from the 1960 to today. Following the economic expansion of the early 1980s, the U.S. current account balance began to rise in the late 1980s and reached its peak in 1991. The year 2008 brought in a serious economic crisis, just as bad as the crisis of 2001, but nowhere near the 1991 levels.

Why does a country's Current Account Balance reflect the economic situation? During the boom phase of the country, the country's currency

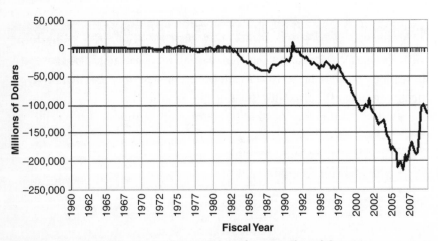

Figure 18   The U.S. Net Current Account Balance from 1960 Through Present

Events this week:

- Revised GDP, first quarter, 2011, U.S.
- Personal Income, U.S.
- Existing Home Sales, May 2011
- Personal Consumption Expenditures for May 2011
- Manufacturers' Shipments, Inventories, and Orders for May 2011
- Unit Auto and Truck Sales for June 2011
- Challenger, Gray & Christmas Employment Report
- Job Opening and Labor Turnover Survey (JOLTS)

Friday, July 1, 2011

Canada Day (Canadian Markets Closed)

7:30 A.M. Challenger, Gray & Christmas Employment Report

10:00 A.M. ISM Report on Business—Manufacturing for June 2011

10:00 A.M. Pending Home Sales Index

10:00 A.M. Construction Spending for May 2011

Notes: _____

_____
_____
_____
_____
_____
_____
_____
_____
_____
_____
_____
_____
_____
_____
_____
_____
_____
_____
_____
_____
_____
_____
_____
_____
_____
_____
_____
_____
_____
_____
_____
_____

strengthens, resulting in cheaper imports and more expensive exports, lowering the Current Account Balance. When the country falls into a recession, the domestic currency weakens, the imports (exports) become less (more) affordable and the Current Account Balance increases.

CURRENT ACCOUNT BALANCE AND THE U.S. DOLLAR

Many economic forces affect the level and the value of the U.S. dollar. The value of the U.S. currency is measured relative to currencies of other countries, as well as to its relative purchasing power of common goods like corn, wheat, oil, precious metals, other commodities, industrial and retail products, and other common products available for sale.

The Current Account Balance is one of the economic influences that impact the value of the U.S. dollar. A quarterly statistic produced by the Bureau of Economic Analysis, the U.S. Current Account Balance report identifies trends in international trade and has three broad categories.

1. Goods and services trade, excluding military items.
2. Income earned on direct investments outside of the United States.
3. Net unilateral transfers of funds, excluding military grants.

Research by Olivier Blanchard, Francesco Giavazzi, and Filipa Sa (*Brookings Papers on Economic Activity*, 2005) shows that different components of the Current Account Balance have different impacts on the strength of the U.S. dollar. Sharp increases in the U.S. imports—increases in the U.S. demand for foreign goods—result in a sharp depreciation of the U.S. dollar, and are followed by additional, more gradual depreciation. On the other hand, sharp increases in foreign holdings of U.S. securities— increases in foreign demand for U.S. assets—at first cause an appreciation of the U.S. dollar, but also cause the U.S. dollar to depreciate in the long term.

According to this analysis, if U.S. imports exceed the exports in the Goods and Services section of the latest Current Account Balance, the U.S. dollar is about to depreciate. In these circumstances, quant investors

JULY 4–10, 2011

Events this week:

- Unit Auto and Truck Sales for June 2011
- Manufacturers' Shipments, Inventories, and Orders for May 2011
- Challenger, Gray & Christmas Employment Report
- Job Opening and Labor Turnover Survey (JOLTS)
- Productivity and Costs

Monday, July 4, 2011

U.S. Independence Day (U.S. Markets Closed)

Tuesday, July 5, 2011

🛒 **7:45 A.M.**   ICSC Retail Sales Index

🛒 **8:55 A.M.**   Johnson Redbook Report

🛒 **5:00 P.M.**   ABC News Consumer Comfort Index

Wednesday, July 6, 2011

🏠 **7:00 A.M.**   U.S. Mortgage Application Indexes

💼 **8:15 A.M.**   ADP National Employment Report

💠 **10:00 A.M.**   ISM Report on Business—Non-Manufacturing for June 2011

Thursday, July 7, 2011

💼 **6:00 A.M.**   Monster Employment Index

💵 **7:00 A.M.**   Bank of England Rate Decision (U.K.)

💵 **7:45 A.M.**   European Central Bank Interest Rate Announcement

💼 **8:30 A.M.**   U.S. Unemployment Insurance Claims

💵 **11:00 A.M.**   13- and 26-Week U.S. T-Bill Auction Announcements

📈 **4:30 P.M.**   U.S. Monetary Aggregates

📈 **4:30 P.M.**   U.S. Monetary Base

Friday, July 8, 2011

💼 **8:30 A.M.**   The Employment Situation

Notes:

JULY

optimally shift at least a portion of their financial portfolio away from the U.S. dollar and the U.S. dollar-denominated assets and into foreign currencies. The authors of the study identify the Euro, Chinese Yuan, and Japanese Yen as the best currencies to diversify one's U.S. dollar exposure.

On the other hand, if the latest Current Account Balance shows a net inflow of foreign capital in Net Unilateral Transfers of Funds, investors may expect a short-term appreciation in the U.S. dollar, followed by a long-term depreciation in the currency. The optimal portfolio allocation then depends on the length of one's investment horizon.

HIGHER INTERNATIONAL TRADE = LOWER U.S. STOCKS

Every month, about five weeks after each month's end, the Bureau of the Census at the U.S. Department of Commerce releases a report on the difference between the U.S. imports and exports of both goods and services. The data are raw monthly numbers, showing the latest snapshot of international trade activity involving the United States.

Figure 19 shows the average response of the S&P 500 to reported month-to-month changes in U.S. international trade. Immediately following an

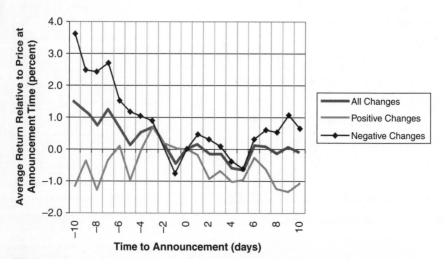

Figure 19   Response of S&P 500 to Changes in Level of the International Trade Balance (United States).

Events this week:

- U.S. NFIB Small Business Optimism Index for June 2011
- Bank of Canada Target Bank Rate Announcement
- U.S. Industrial Production and Capacity Utilization for June 2011
- U.S. Retail Sales for June 2011
- U.S. Manufacturing and Trade Inventories and Sales for May 2011
- Housing Starts and Building Permits for June 2011
- International Trade Balance for May 2011
- Treasury International Capital Flows for May 2011
- Consumer Price Index
- Producer Price Index
- Productivity and Costs
- Import and Export Prices

Monday, July 11, 2011

11:00 A.M.   U.S. Treasury Bill Auction Announcement

Tuesday, July 12, 2011

7:45 A.M.   ICSC Retail Sales Index

8:55 A.M.   Johnson Redbook Report

5:00 P.M.   ABC News Consumer Comfort Index

Wednesday, July 13, 2011

7:00 A.M.   U.S. Mortgage Application Indexes

2:00 P.M.   U.S. Federal Budget Balance

Thursday, July 14, 2011

8:30 A.M.   U.S. Unemployment Insurance Claims

11:00 A.M.   13- and 26-Week U.S. T-Bill Auction Announcements

4:30 P.M.   U.S. Monetary Aggregates

4:30 P.M.   U.S. Monetary Base

Friday, July 15, 2011

8:30 A.M.   Empire State Manufacturing Survey

10:00 A.M.   U.S. Consumer Sentiment, preliminary data

12:00 P.M.   July 2011 options expire

Notes:

JULY

increase in the International Trade figures, the S&P 500 declines, and vice versa.

The effect of changes in the International Trade may not be as pronounced as that of other indexes. The U.S. customs receipts data for the same month is made available by the U.S. Treasury about four weeks prior to release of international trade figures. As a result, market prices already incorporate at least some of the international trade information by the time the official announcement is made by the Bureau of Census.

TICS AND FOREIGN EXCHANGE INVESTING

Since 1978, the Treasury International Capital System (TICS) provides monthly data on investments movement into and out of the United States.

This monthly report reviews the balance of purchases and sales of long-term U.S. and foreign securities made by the U.S. entities and those of foreign nations. The scope of the report includes equities and fixed income securities maturing in at least one year. TICS flows affect the demand and supply for given currencies, and the statistics influence the value of the U.S. dollar relative to other world currencies.

Figure 20 shows the average response of GBP/USD to changes in TICS. When TICS rises (demand for foreign bonds outstrips demand for U.S.

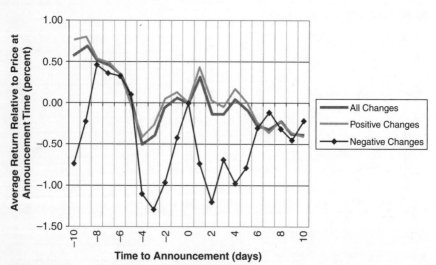

Figure 20   Response of the U.K. Pound Sterling/U.S. Dollar Exchange Rate (GBP/USD) to Changes in the U.S. TICS Figures.

Events this week:

- U.S. Durable Goods Orders for June 2011
- Bank of Canada Target Bank Rate Announcement
- Composite Index of Leading Economic Indicators for June 2011
- Housing Starts and Building Permits for June 2011

Monday, July 18, 2011

Marine Day (Japan Markets Closed)

- 11:00 A.M.   U.S. Treasury Bill Auction Announcement

Tuesday, July 19, 2011

- 7:45 A.M.   ICSC Retail Sales Index
- 8:55 A.M.   Johnson Redbook Report
- 5:00 P.M.   ABC News Consumer Comfort Index

Wednesday, July 20, 2011

- 7:00 A.M.   U.S. Mortgage Application Indexes
- 7:00 A.M.   Bank of England Minutes of the Monetary Policy Committee (U.K.)

Thursday, July 21, 2011

- 8:30 A.M.   U.S. Unemployment Insurance Claims
- 10:00 A.M.   Philadelphia Fed Business Outlook Survey
- 11:00 A.M.   13- and 26-Week U.S. T-Bill Auction Announcements
- 4:30 P.M.   U.S. Monetary Aggregates
- 4:30 P.M.   U.S. Monetary Base

Friday, July 22, 2011

Notes:

JULY

bonds), the British currency rises. At the same time, when TICS falls, the
U.S. dollar rises and the foreign currency falls.

FOREIGN FLOWS INTO U.S. BONDS
LOWER U.S. INTEREST RATES

A component of the U.S. Treasury International Capital System (TICS)
report is foreign flows into U.S. bonds. According to the research of
Francis and Veronica Warnock (*Journal of International Money and Finance*, 2009), foreign flows into U.S. bonds are an important driver of bond
prices and their yields. While the Monetary Committee of the U.S. Federal
Reserve largely determines the levels of U.S. interest rates, the authors of
the study estimate that annual foreign inflows into U.S. bonds lower the
10-year Treasury yield by at least 1.5 percent per year. As a result, changes
in TICS levels can help predict future long-term bond rates.

U.S. interest rates are determined as follows: The U.S. Federal Reserve
(the Fed) decides on a "target" interest rate at which it lends to banks, thus
setting the minimum rate for all lending activity in the country. To finance
its lending to banks, the Fed issues U.S. bonds with different interest rates
and maturities. Yet, the Fed is not alone in controlling the long-term rates in
the U.S. economy. Once the Fed bonds hit the open markets, market supply

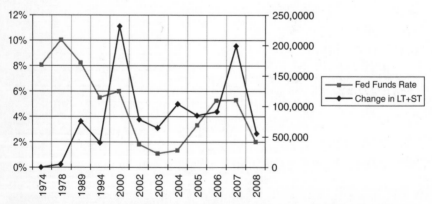

Figure 21   The Relationship between the U.S. Federal Funds Rate (Left Scale) and the
Change in Foreign Holdings of Long-term and Short-term U.S. Debt.

Events this week:

- Advance GDP Figures, second quarter 2011, U.S.
- Advance Personal Income, second quarter 2011, U.S.
- Manufacturers' Shipments, Inventories, and Orders for June 2011
- Personal Consumption Expenditures for June 2011
- U.S. Durable Goods Orders for June 2011
- Housing Vacancies and Homeownership Rates
- PCE- and GDP-Based Price Indexes for June 2011
- Employment Cost Index for second quarter 2011

Monday, July 25, 2011

🏠	10:00 A.M.	Existing Home Sales for June 2011
💰	11:00 A.M.	U.S. Treasury Bill Auction Announcement

Tuesday, July 26, 2011

🛒	7:45 A.M.	ICSC Retail Sales Index
🛒	8:55 A.M.	Johnson Redbook Report
🏠	9:00 A.M.	S&P/Case-Shiller Home Price Indexes for June 2011
🛒	10:00 A.M.	Consumer Confidence
🌐	10:00 A.M.	Richmond Federal Reserve Bank Survey for June 2011
🛒	5:00 A.M.	ABC News Consumer Comfort Index

Wednesday, July 27, 2011

🏠	7:00 A.M.	U.S. Mortgage Application Indexes
🌐	2:00 P.M.	Current Economic Conditions ("Beige Book")

Thursday, July 28, 2011

💼	8:30 A.M.	U.S. Unemployment Insurance Claims
💼	10:00 A.M.	Help Wanted Advertising Index for June 2011
🌐	11:00 A.M.	Kansas City Federal Reserve Bank Manufacturing Survey for June 2011
💰	11:00 A.M.	13- and 26-Week U.S. T-Bill Auction Announcements
📈	4:30 P.M.	U.S. Monetary Aggregates
📈	4:30 P.M.	U.S. Monetary Base

Friday, July 29, 2011

🌐	9:45 A.M.	Chicago Business Barometer
🛒	10:00 A.M.	U.S. Consumer Sentiment, final data

Notes: _____

JULY

and demand control their yield (the higher the demand for bonds, the higher the bond prices, the lower the yield). The Fed then takes the market bond yield into consideration when deciding upon future interest rate changes. A monthly increase in TICS signals higher demand for the U.S. bonds and thus forecasts lower interest rates.

As Figure 21 (on page 100) shows, however, the relationship between TICS and U.S. interest rates can be a two-way street. While the foreign demand for U.S. long-term bonds affects the Fed Fund rates, the Fed Fund rates shape foreign demand for all U.S. securities, equities, and debt, short and long-term. The higher the Fed Fund rates, the higher the short-term bond rate, the higher the U.S. return on equities and debt, and the higher the foreign demand for the U.S. securities.

EMPLOYMENT

Sun	Mon	Tue	Wed	Thu	Fri	Sat
	1	2	3	4	5	6
7	8	9	10	11	12	13
14	15	16	17	18	19	20
21	22	23	24	25	26	27
28	29	30	31			

KEY HIGHLIGHTS

Employment can be a key variable in quantitative investing. This month's articles deal with the following topics.

- Employment as an Economic Indicator
- Which Employment Index is Best?
- ADP Employment Report
- The Employment Situation
- Challenger, Gray & Christmas Employment Report

AUGUST

103

EMPLOYMENT AS AN ECONOMIC INDICATOR

Several economic indexes, some reported monthly and some quarterly, are designed to illustrate concurrent economic conditions through U.S. employment.

Each index attempts to measure employment in a slightly different way, giving investors a wide spectrum of information to work with. Some of the more popular employment indexes and their descriptions are summarized in Table 5 (on page 106).

WHICH EMPLOYMENT INDEX IS BEST?

It's not a secret that a healthy economy is capable of employing more people than weak economy. The level and trending in employment, therefore, wield a significant influence in quantitative analysis of economic conditions and securities markets.

When analyzing the impact of employment metrics on financial securities every quantitative investor is confronted with the same question: Which employment indicator is best to use?

Different employment statistics are designed to illuminate numerous facets of the country's economic health through that of the workforce. As a result, there are several factors to keep in mind when selecting the employment measures to incorporate into a trading strategy.

- Frequency of reporting
- Historic reaction of security markets to announcements
- Noise in the data

FREQUENCY OF REPORTING

As a rule of thumb, indexes that are reported more frequently provide a here-and-now picture of the employment situation and have more relevance to the current economic conditions. The timeliness of the information

Events this week:

- Pending Home Sales Index
- Challenger, Gray & Christmas Employment Report
- Unit Auto and Truck Sales for July 2011
- Manufacturers' Shipments, Inventories, and Orders for June 2011
- Job Opening and Labor Turnover Survey (JOLTS)

Monday, August 1, 2011

	10:00 A.M.	ISM Report on Business—Manufacturing for July 2011
	10:00 A.M.	Construction Spending for June 2011
	11:00 A.M.	U.S. Treasury Bill Auction Announcement

Tuesday, August 2, 2011

	7:45 A.M.	ICSC Retail Sales Index
	8:55 A.M.	Johnson Redbook Report
	5:00 P.M.	ABC News Consumer Comfort Index

Wednesday, August 3, 2011

	7:00 A.M.	U.S. Mortgage Application Indexes
	8:15 A.M.	ADP National Employment Report
	10:00 A.M.	ISM Report on Business—Non-Manufacturing for July 2010

Thursday, August 4, 2011

	6:00 A.M.	Monster Employment Index
	7:00 A.M.	Bank of England Rate Decision (U.K.)
	7:45 A.M.	European Central Bank Interest Rate Announcement
	8:30 A.M.	U.S. Unemployment Insurance Claims
	10:00 A.M.	OFHEO Home Price Index, U.S.
	11:00 A.M.	13- and 26-Week U.S. T-Bill Auction Announcements
	4:30 P.M.	U.S. Monetary Aggregates
	4:30 P.M.	U.S. Monetary Base

Friday, August 5, 2011

	8:30 A.M.	The Employment Situation

Notes:

AUGUST

Table 5   Employment Indexes

Index	Description
The Current Population Survey	Determines the U.S. unemployment level based on interviews of individual households.
The Current Employment Statistics Survey	Determines the U.S. unemployment level from the non-farm payroll data.
ADP Employment Report	This report is an estimate of monthly changes in private-sector non-farm employment observed through payrolls of ADP clients.
Challenger, Gray & Christmas Employment Report	This report aggregates the numbers of corporate layoffs reported across the U.S. during the previous month.
Help Wanted Advertising Index	The number of help-wanted advertisements, measured as lines of print, in the classified sections of 51 U.S. newspapers.
Monster Employment Index	Monster Employment Index is compiled from online Help Wanted advertisements posted on Monster.com website.
Manpower Employment Outlook Survey	An employment forecast based on a quarterly survey by Manpower Inc. of the firm's clients.
Business Employment Dynamics	This survey, produced by the Bureau of Labor Statistics at the U.S. Department of Labor, reports the number of jobs created or lost as identified in the latest Quarterly Census of Employment and Wages.
Unemployment Insurance Claims	This report produces the numbers of initial claims and the numbers of continuing claims. Initial claims are reported with a five-day lag, and continuing claims are accounted for 12 days after the claims are recorded.
Job Opening and Labor Turnover Survey	The Job Opening and Labor Turnover Survey (JOLTS) reports shortages and turnover in the U.S. job market. The survey is prepared by the Bureau of Labor Statistics.

is balanced with the reality that small changes over a short period of time may not reflect a secular trend.

Indexes reported less frequently, say, quarterly, often aggregate the past months' data and can be less influential as a result. The trends in quarterly data, for example, often exclude very short-term aberrations in

Events this week:

- U.S. NFIB Small Business Optimism Index for July 2011
- U.S. Industrial Production and Capacity Utilization for July 2011
- U.S. Manufacturing and Trade Inventories and Sales for June 2011
- U.S. Retail Sales for July 2011
- International Trade Balance for June 2011
- Treasury International Capital Flows for June 2011
- Job Opening and Labor Turnover Survey (JOLTS)
- Consumer Price Index
- Productivity and Costs
- Import and Export Prices

Monday, August 8, 2011

	11:00 A.M.	U.S. Treasury Bill Auction Announcement

Tuesday, August 9, 2011

	7:45 A.M.	ICSC Retail Sales Index
	8:55 A.M.	Johnson Redbook Report
	5:00 P.M.	ABC News Consumer Comfort Index

Wednesday, August 10, 2011

	7:00 A.M.	U.S. Mortgage Application Indexes
	7:00 A.M.	Bank of England Inflation Report (U.K.)
	2:00 P.M.	U.S. Federal Budget Balance

Thursday, August 11, 2011

	8:30 A.M.	U.S. Unemployment Insurance Claims
	11:00 A.M.	13- and 26-Week U.S. T-Bill Auction Announcements
	4:30 P.M.	U.S. Monetary Aggregates
	4:30 P.M.	U.S. Monetary Base

Friday, August 12, 2011

	8:30 A.M.	The Employment Situation
	10:00 A.M.	U.S. Consumer Sentiment, preliminary data

Notes:

AUGUST

the statistics. Yet, trading on oft-reported indicators requires frequent analysis reevaluating security positions. The longer the duration of the quant investor's position holding horizon, the less frequently reported indicators the investor is likely to use.

CAPABILITY TO LEAD FINANCIAL SECURITY MARKETS

Forward-looking indicators, such as outlook surveys, provide forward-looking sentiment that may move markets. At the same time, outlook surveys are subjective opinions of market participants and do not always translate into actual figures. In contrast, figures compiled based on past information are more reliable, but may also be already priced in by the markets, reducing their usefulness in quantitative investing.

ACCURACY OF DATA

Some of the fluctuations in all employment indexes are due to demographic and other factors unrelated to the state of the economy, and they are not likely to affect financial securities. Different indexes may be accompanied by various adjustments, such as adjustments for the season of the year, demographic profile, industry, and geographic region from which the survey results were obtained.

While the U.S. unemployment rate, released as part of the Employment Situation report, is often considered an accurate and key indicator for the state of employment, the Unemployment Insurance Claims report, released every week, is also carefully followed to assess the immediate quantitative impact on securities.

ADP EMPLOYMENT REPORT

Automatic Data Processing, Inc., (ADP) processes payrolls for nearly 23 million workers employed by 400,000 businesses in the United States. With such a wide reach, ADP collects unique insights into the employment situation in the country, incorporating all firm sizes and industries.

Events this week:

- U.S. Durable Goods Orders for July 2011
- U.S. Industrial Production and Capacity Utilization for July 2011
- Composite Index of Leading Economic Indicators for July 2011
- U.S. Retail Sales for July 2011
- Housing Starts and Building Permits for July 2011
- Treasury International Capital Flows for June 2011
- Consumer Price Index
- Producer Price Index
- Productivity and Costs

Monday, August 15, 2011

8:30 A.M. Empire State Manufacturing Survey

11:00 A.M. U.S. Treasury Bill Auction Announcement

Tuesday, August 16, 2011

7:45 A.M. ICSC Retail Sales Index

8:55 A.M. Johnson Redbook Report

5:00 P.M. ABC News Consumer Comfort Index

Wednesday, August 17, 2011

7:00 A.M. U.S. Mortgage Application Indexes

7:00 A.M. Bank of England Minutes of the Monetary Policy Committee (U.K.)

Thursday, August 18, 2011

8:30 A.M. U.S. Unemployment Insurance Claims

10:00 A.M. Philadelphia Fed Business Outlook Survey

11:00 A.M. 13- and 26-Week U.S. T-Bill Auction Announcements

4:30 P.M. U.S. Monetary Aggregates

4:30 P.M. U.S. Monetary Base

Friday, August 19, 2011

8:30 A.M. The Employment Situation

12:00 P.M. August 2011 options expire

Notes:

AUGUST

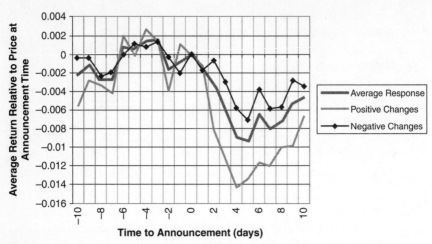

Figure 22   Response of the U.K. Pound Sterling/ U.S. Dollar Exchange Rate (GBP/USD) to Changes in the U.S. ADP Employment Report.

The ADP Employment Report is an estimate of monthly changes in private-sector nonfarm payrolls. It is designed to accurately quantify several facets of information collected by ADP. In particular, the index is thought to quickly echo expansions in hiring as well as the formation of new businesses. The report is released monthly at 8:15 A.M. E.T. two days prior to the release of the Employment Situation report produced by the U.S. government.

A rise (fall) in reported payrolls may signal economic expansion (contraction). Figure 22 shows average responses of the GBP/USD exchange rate to all positive and negative changes in the ADP Employment figures. As Figure 22 shows, rising employment in the United States tends to increases the value of USD relative to that of GBP, depressing the GBP/USD rate. Surprisingly, negative changes in ADP Employment figures also reduce GBP/USD, albeit to a much smaller extent. To trade GBP/USD on changes in the ADP Employment Report, sell GBP/USD (buy USD) when the report shows a positive change in U.S. employment.

THE EMPLOYMENT SITUATION

The Employment Situation provides lagging information about the U.S. labor market, including statistics on employment, unemployment, and

AUGUST 22-28, 2011

Events this week:

- Preliminary GDP Figures, second quarter 2011, U.S.
- Preliminary Personal Income, second quarter 2011, U.S.
- Preliminary Corporate Profits, second quarter 2011, U.S.
- U.S. Durable Goods Orders for July 2011
- Personal Consumption Expenditures for July 2011
- PCE- and GDP-Based Price Indexes for July 2011
- Employment Cost Index for second quarter 2011

Monday, August 22, 2011

11:00 A.M.   U.S. Treasury Bill Auction Announcement

Tuesday, August 23, 2011

7:45 A.M.   ICSC Retail Sales Index

8:55 A.M.   Johnson Redbook Report

10:00 A.M.   Richmond Federal Reserve Bank Survey for July 2011

5:00 P.M.   ABC News Consumer Comfort Index

Wednesday, August 24, 2011

7:00 A.M.   U.S. Mortgage Application Indexes

Thursday, August 25, 2011

8:30 A.M.   U.S. Unemployment Insurance Claims

10:00 A.M.   Existing Home Sales for July 2011

10:00 A.M.   Help Wanted Advertising Index for July 2011

11:00 A.M.   Kansas City Federal Reserve Bank Manufacturing Survey for July 2011

11:00 A.M.   13- and 26-Week U.S. T-Bill Auction Announcements

4:30 P.M.   U.S. Monetary Aggregates

4:30 P.M.   U.S. Monetary Base

Friday, August 26, 2011

10:00 A.M.   U.S. Consumer Sentiment, preliminary data

Notes: _____

AUGUST

wage earnings. This report has comprehensive statistics on the employment and unemployment of Americans, and its details give insights about
the degree to which the economy is expanding or contracting. The report
often (but not always) has a significant effect on the markets the day it is
released.

The report contains two surveys:

1. The Current Population Survey, also known as the "household survey,"
   is based on interviews of individual households.
2. The Current Employment Statistics Survey, referred to as the
   "establishment survey," is determined from the nonfarm payroll data.

The household survey has a more expansive scope than the establishment survey because it includes the self-employed, unpaid family workers,
agricultural workers, and private household workers, who are excluded by
the establishment survey. The household survey also provides estimates of
employment by demographic groups.

Figure 23 shows the response of the Utilities sector ETF (ticker: XLU) to
changes in Employment Situation figures. Rising unemployment detected
by the Employment Situation index results in a small decline in the price of
XLU, whereas falling unemployment on average causes a dramatic upswing
in the stock price of XLU.

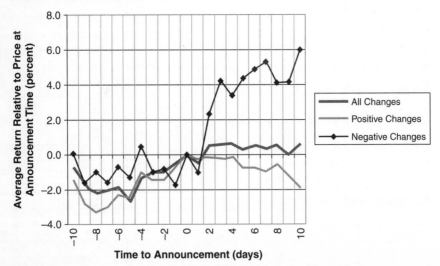

Figure 23   Response of XLU to Changes in the U.S. Employment Situation report.

Events this week:

- Preliminary GDP Figures, second quarter 2011, U.S.
- Preliminary Personal Income, second quarter 2011, U.S.
- Preliminary Corporate Profits, second quarter 2011, U.S.
- Pending Home Sales Index, U.S.
- Challenger, Gray & Christmas Employment Report
- Bank of Canada Target Bank Rate Announcement
- Manufacturers' Shipments, Inventories, and Orders for July 2011
- Personal Consumption Expenditures for July 2011
- PCE- and GDP-Based Price Indexes for July 2011

Monday, August 29, 2011

💵	11:00 A.M.	U.S. Treasury Bill Auction Announcement

Tuesday, August 30, 2011

🛒	7:45 A.M.	ICSC Retail Sales Index
🛒	8:55 A.M.	Johnson Redbook Report
🏠	9:00 A.M.	S&P/Case-Shiller Home Price Indexes for July 2011
🛒	10:00 A.M.	Consumer Confidence
🛒	5:00 P.M.	ABC News Consumer Comfort Index

Wednesday, August 31, 2011

🏠	7:00 A.M.	U.S. Mortgage Application Indexes
💼	8:15 A.M.	ADP National Employment Report
⚙	9:45 A.M.	Chicago Business Barometer

Notes: _____

_____
_____
_____
_____
_____
_____
_____
_____
_____
_____
_____
_____
_____
_____
_____
_____
_____
_____
_____
_____
_____
_____
_____
_____
_____
_____
_____
_____
_____

AUG/SEP

CHALLENGER, GRAY & CHRISTMAS
EMPLOYMENT REPORT

The Challenger, Gray & Christmas Employment Report, also known as the Challenger Job-Cut Report, aggregates the numbers of corporate layoffs reported across the United States during the previous month. A positive change in the report indicates that more workers were eliminated during the past month in comparison with the previous month.

Challenger, Gray & Christmas, Inc. is a U.S. outplacement consulting firm. Founded in the early 1960s, the firm assists recently laid-off workers of all levels to find new jobs. Through its displaced clients, the firm collects information about most recent layoffs in various industries. This information then serves as a basis for their Challenger, Gray & Christmas Employment Report index.

As expected, the U.S. markets react negatively to increases in job cuts. As Figure 24 shows, the S&P 500 index experiences a sharp decline following increases in job cuts, registered by rising Challenger, Gray & Christmas Index. A tradable strategy, therefore, can be to short S&P 500 immediately after an announcement of increases in job cuts.

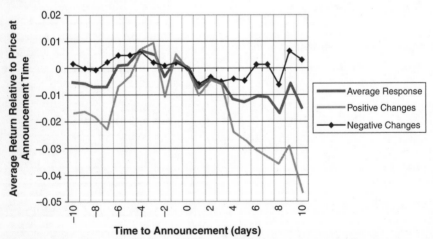

Figure 24   Response of S&P 500 to Changes in the Challenger Job-Cut Report.

PRICES, WAGES, AND PRODUCTIVITY

SEPTEMBER 2011

Sun	Mon	Tue	Wed	Thu	Fri	Sat
				1	2	3
4	5	6	7	8	9	10
11	12	13	14	15	16	17
18	19	20	21	22	23	24
25	26	27	28	29	30	

KEY HIGHLIGHTS

Prices, wages, and productivity are some of the key ingredients determining the economic welfare of a country. This month's articles deal with the following topics and their effects on the markets.

- Consumer Price Index
- Producer Price Index
- Import and Export Prices
- Employment Cost Index
- News on Productivity Drives Markets; The Productivity and Costs Index Does Not

SEPTEMBER

CONSUMER PRICE INDEX

The Consumer Price Index (CPI) is one of the core indicators of rising or falling inflation. The U.S. monthly CPI tracks a basket of goods and services that consumers regularly buy in the United States.

There are about 80,000 price data points that go into the CPI computation every month. Table 6 shows the breakdown of the CPI into its components.

Table 6   CPI Components

Component of the CPI	Weight of the Component in the CPI	
	Total CPI	Core CPI
Housing	42.7%	49.5%
Shelter	32.8%	42.3%
Owner's equivalent rent	23.8%	30.8%
Rent of primary residence	5.9%	7.7%
Lodging away from home	2.6%	3.4%
Tenants and household insurance	0.4%	0.5%
Fuel and utilities	5.3%	1.2%
Household furnishings and operations	4.7%	6.0%
Food and beverages	15.0%	1.4%
Transportation	17.2%	17.4%
New vehicles	5.0%	6.4%
Other private transportation	11.2%	15.3%
Motor fuel	4.3%	
Maintenance and repairs	1.1%	1.5%
Used cars and trucks	1.7%	2.2%
Public transportation	1.1%	1.4%
Medical care	6.3%	8.1%
Apparel	3.7%	4.8%
Recreation	5.6%	7.2%
Education and communication	6.0%	7.8%
Other goods and services	3.5%	4.5%
Tobacco and smoking products	0.7%	0.9%

Source: U.S. Department of Labor.

AUGUST 29–SEPTEMBER 4, 2011

Events this week:

- Preliminary GDP, second quarter 2011, U.S.
- Corporate Profits, second quarter 2011, U.S.
- Personal Income, U.S.
- Pending Home Sales Index, U.S.
- Challenger, Gray & Christmas Employment Report
- Unit Auto and Truck Sales for August 2011
- Manufacturers' Shipments, Inventories, and Orders for July 2011
- Job Opening and Labor Turnover Survey (JOLTS)

Thursday, September 1, 2011

6:00 A.M.	Monster Employment Index
8:30 A.M.	U.S. Unemployment Insurance Claims
10:00 A.M.	ISM Report on Business—Manufacturing for August 2011
10:00 A.M.	Construction Spending for July 2011
11:00 A.M.	13- and 26-Week U.S. T-Bill Auction Announcements
4:30 P.M.	U.S. Monetary Aggregates
4:30 P.M.	U.S. Monetary Base

Friday, September 2, 2011

8:30 A.M.	The Employment Situation

Notes:

AUG/SEP

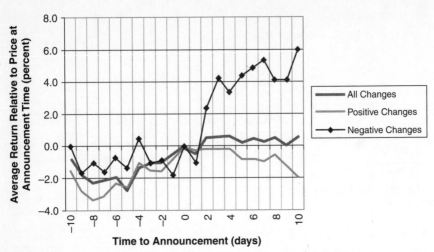

Figure 25   Response of COKE to Changes in the U.S. Consumer Price Index.

Changes in the U.S. CPI are closely watched and move the U.S. markets. According to economic theories, the optimal CPI growth equals that of population growth, and is about 2 percent per year in equilibrium. As a result, rising CPI is expected by many market participants and causes a less pronounced response in the markets than does falling inflation. Figure 25 illustrates this phenomenon with the example of Coca-Cola shock (COKE).

Over time, announcements of declines in CPI are coincident with COKE shares soaring, while the shares fall moderately following announcements of rising CPI.

PRODUCER PRICE INDEX

The Producer Price Index (PPI) is a group of indexes that report on the prices that manufacturers receive for goods that they have sold. Three different indexes of producer prices are reported monthly.

1. *The PPI for finished goods:* Products ready to be shipped to wholesalers and retailers.

Events this week:

- Manufacturers' Shipments, Inventories, and Orders for July 2011
- International Trade Balance for July 2011
- Challenger, Gray & Christmas Employment Report
- Job Opening and Labor Turnover Survey (JOLTS)
- Productivity and Costs
- Import and Export Prices
- Flow of Funds

Monday, September 5, 2011

U.S. Labor Day (U.S. Markets Closed)

Tuesday, September 6, 2011

🛒	7:45 A.M.	ICSC Retail Sales Index
🛒	8:55 A.M.	Johnson Redbook Report
⊕	10:00 A.M.	ISM Report on Business—Non-Manufacturing for August 2010
🛒	5:00 P.M.	ABC News Consumer Comfort Index

Wednesday, September 7, 2011

🏠	7:00 A.M.	U.S. Mortgage Application Indexes

Thursday, September 8, 2011

	7:00 A.M.	Bank of England Rate Decision (U.K.)
	7:45 A.M.	European Central Bank Interest Rate Announcement
	8:30 A.M.	U.S. Unemployment Insurance Claims
	11:00 A.M.	13- and 26-Week U.S. T-Bill Auction Announcements
	4:30 P.M.	U.S. Monetary Aggregates
	4:30 P.M.	U.S. Monetary Base

Friday, September 9, 2011

Notes:

SEPTEMBER

Table 7   PPI Breakdown for Finished Goods

	Finished Goods PPI
Food and Beverages	21.5%
Other consumer nondurables	38.5%
Apparel and footwear	1.7%
Gasoline	5.3%
Residential natural gas	3.0%
Residential electric power	7.8%
Tobacco products	1.8%
Other	18.8%
Consumer durable goods	15.9%
Passenger cars	4.1%
Other	11.8%
Capital equipment	24.0%
Light motor trucks	6.4%
Other	17.7%

2. *The PPI for intermediate goods, supplies, and components:* Products that are not yet finished but are in the production process.

3. *The PPI for crude materials that require further processing:* Raw materials and commodities

Table 7 shows the breakdown of PPI for finished goods.

Like CPI, PPI tends to significantly influence the U.S markets and the U.S. dollar. Figure 26 (on page 122) shows the average response of the British pound sterling/U.S. dollar exchange rate (ticker: GBP/USD) to changes in the U.S. PPI. The lower the PPI, the higher the U.S. dollar, the lower the value of GBP/USD.

Import and Export Prices

Import and export prices are indicators of international economic activity and competitiveness in world markets. In the United States, the Bureau of Labor Statistics has reported on import and export prices monthly since 1989. These price indexes measure the relative changes of prices of goods

Events this week:

- U.S. NFIB Small Business Optimism Index for August 2011
- U.S. Durable Goods Orders for August 2011
- U.S. Industrial Production and Capacity Utilization for August 2011
- U.S. Manufacturing and Trade Inventories and Sales for July 2011
- U.S. Retail Sales for August 2011
- Housing Starts and Building Permits for August 2011
- International Trade Balance for July 2011
- Current Account Balance, second quarter 2011
- Treasury International Capital Flows for July 2011
- Consumer Price Index
- Producer Price Index
- Productivity and Costs
- Flow of Funds

Monday, September 12, 2011

	11:00 A.M.	U.S. Treasury Bill Auction Announcement

Tuesday, September 13, 2011

	12:01 A.M.	Manpower Employment Outlook Survey
	7:45 A.M.	ICSC Retail Sales Index
	8:55 A.M.	Johnson Redbook Report
	2:00 P.M.	U.S. Federal Budget Balance
	5:00 P.M.	ABC News Consumer Comfort Index

Wednesday, September 14, 2011

	7:00 A.M.	U.S. Mortgage Application Indexes
	2:00 P.M.	Current Economic Conditions ("Beige Book")

Thursday, September 15, 2011

	8:30 A.M.	Empire State Manufacturing Survey
	8:30 A.M.	U.S. Unemployment Insurance Claims
	10:00 A.M.	Philadelphia Fed Business Outlook Survey
	11:00 A.M.	13- and 26-Week U.S. T-Bill Auction Announcements
	4:30 P.M.	U.S. Monetary Aggregates
	4:30 P.M.	U.S. Monetary Base

Friday, September 16, 2011

	10:00 A.M.	U.S. Consumer Sentiment, preliminary data
	12:00 P.M.	September 2011 options expire

Notes:

SEPTEMBER

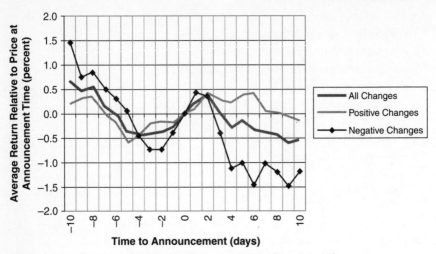

Figure 26   Response of GBP/USD to Changes in U.S. Producer Price Index.

exported to other countries and imported from abroad. The price of imported goods is an ingredient in the expectations about future inflation,
especially relating to petroleum products. The report on U.S. import and
export prices can also provide insight about the evolving competitiveness
of U.S. products in foreign markets.

Classic economic models imply that free trade stimulates a country's
economic prosperity. The economists subscribing to this view argue that
free markets are perfectly self-regulating mechanisms, adjusting prices to
shocks and reflecting the market participants' collective beliefs and information. According to classic free-market theories, countries naturally
specialize in producing goods that best fit their "competitive advantage,"
where a competitive advantage can be the country's proximity to water,
annual amount of sunshine, natural dexterity of its people, to name a few.
The classicists then argue that government intervention only complicates
matters and introduces frictions and other inefficiencies, precluding markets from working in their most optimal manner.

A number of more recent models, however, defend "interventionism," a government interference to further improve domestic economies.
These models argue that governments can intervene strategically
to enhance their competitive position. Government tools of market

SEPTEMBER 19–25, 2011

Events this week:

- Existing Home Sales for August 2011
- U.S. Durable Goods Orders for August 2011
- Composite Index of Leading Economic Indicators for August 2011
- Housing Starts and Building Permits for August 2011

Monday, September 19, 2011

Respect for the Aged Day (Japan Markets Closed)

11:00 A.M.   U.S. Treasury Bill Auction Announcement

Tuesday, September 20, 2011

7:45 A.M.   ICSC Retail Sales Index

8:55 A.M.   Johnson Redbook Report

5:00 P.M.   ABC News Consumer Comfort Index

Wednesday, September 21, 2011

7:00 A.M.   U.S. Mortgage Application Indexes

7:00 A.M.   Bank of England Minutes of the Monetary Policy
             Committee (U.K.)

Thursday, September 22, 2011

8:30 A.M.   U.S. Unemployment Insurance Claims

11:00 A.M.   13- and 26-Week U.S. T-Bill Auction Announcements

4:30 P.M.   U.S. Monetary Aggregates

4:30 P.M.   U.S. Monetary Base

Friday, September 23, 2011

Autumn Equinox (Japan Markets Closed)

Notes: _____

SEPTEMBER

intervention include domestic subsidies, tax breaks for exporters, tariffs and other barriers for importers. The interventionists argue that import restrictions, export subsidies and tax breaks help domestic growth. When the government imposes extra tariffs on imports, for example, import prices tend to rise to offset the importers' expense.* Higher prices on imports, in turn, make the imports less competitive with domestic products, stimulating demand for domestic goods, and ultimately having a positive affect on the economy. See, for example, recent research on the topic by Mihir Desai and James Hines (*Journal of International Economics*, 2007).

No clear relationship exists between import prices and the U.S. markets, however. Since 1989, for every percentage point rise (fall) in the monthly U.S. import prices less that month's inflation, the S&P 500 index on average declined (rose) by 4 percent in the same month. After 2001, however, this relationship appears to have reversed itself: For every percentage point rise (fall) in the monthly U.S. import prices adjusted for U.S. inflation, the S&P 500 on average rose (fell) by 1.7 percent within the same month.

Yet, changes in import prices have been shown to forecast future changes in domestic inflation. A one percent rise (fall) in import prices translates into a 0.02 percent rise (fall) in inflation the following month, after import price changes are announced. In this respect, monthly changes in import prices can help to model future movements of securities.

EMPLOYMENT COST INDEX

The quarterly Employment Cost Index (ECI) measures changes in wages for all hourly workers except those involved with the U.S. federal government. The index includes sales commissions but not stock option compensation. The Bureau of Labor Statistics at the U.S. Department of Labor reports this information.

As Figure 27 (on page 126) shows, the ECI generally lags changes observed in the stock market by at least one quarter. Only after the economy advances and the U.S. corporate sector becomes more confident in a new stage of the business cycle, do firms ramp up their hiring and subsequently raise employee compensation.

---

*Note that import prices also tend to rise when the domestic currency weakens.

Events this week:

- Revised GDP Figures, second quarter 2011, U.S.
- Revised Personal Income, second quarter 2011, U.S.
- Revised Corporate Profits, second quarter 2011, U.S.
- Existing Home Sales for August 2011
- Manufacturers' Shipments, Inventories, and Orders for August 2011
- Personal Consumption Expenditures for August 2011
- U.S. Durable Goods Orders for August 2011
- PCE- and GDP-Based Price Indexes for August 2011

Monday, September 26, 2011

	11:00 A.M.	U.S. Treasury Bill Auction Announcement

Tuesday, September 27, 2011

	7:45 A.M.	ICSC Retail Sales Index
	8:55 A.M.	Johnson Redbook Report
	9:00 A.M.	S&P/Case-Shiller Home Price Indexes for August 2011
	10:00 A.M.	Richmond Federal Reserve Bank Survey for August 2011
	10:00 A.M.	Consumer Confidence
	5:00 P.M.	ABC News Consumer Comfort Index

Wednesday, September 28, 2011

	7:00 A.M.	U.S. Mortgage Application Indexes

Thursday, September 29, 2011

	8:30 A.M.	U.S. Unemployment Insurance Claims
	10:00 A.M.	Help Wanted Advertising Index for August 2011
	11:00 A.M.	Kansas City Federal Reserve Bank Manufacturing Survey for August 2011
	11:00 A.M.	13- and 26-Week U.S. T-Bill Auction Announcements
	4:30 P.M.	U.S. Monetary Aggregates
	4:30 P.M.	U.S. Monetary Base

Friday, September 30, 2011

	9:45 A.M.	Chicago Business Barometer
	10:00 A.M.	U.S. Consumer Sentiment, preliminary data

Notes:

SEP/OCT

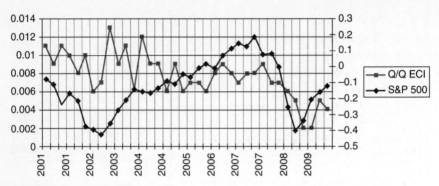

Figure 27   ECI and S&P 500.

However, unexpected changes in ECI (changes above or below expected levels, projected by economists ahead of each ECI announcement) appear to significantly affect the markets on the day of the announcement. Specifically, Refet Gurkaynak, Brian Sack, and Eric Swanson (*International Journal of Central Banking*, 2005) estimate that a 1 percent increase in ECI above the economists' projections consistently occur at the same time as 1-year forward Treasury rates increasing by 3 percent, 5-year forward Treasury rates by 4 percent, and 10-year forward Treasury rates by nearly 4 percent. Yet, these changes in the forward rates occur only over the day immediately following the ECI announcement.

News on Productivity Drives Markets; The Productivity and Costs Index Does Not

The quarterly Productivity and Costs Index (PCI) measures changes in the aggregate output per hour of work. The aggregate output is computed as GDP less private and government output.

While the PCI presents an important measure of technological progress, it is not very useful in predicting the direction of the markets. According to Paul Beadry and Franck Portier (*The American Economic Review*, 2006), the financial markets react more to the news about future technological opportunities rather than by realized gains in productivity. By the time productivity numbers show improvement in work processes, the financial markets look forward to future opportunities to enhance workers' capabilities.

Interestingly, announcements of falling costs of international trade make for good productivity news in a wide range of industries. According to a study by Andrew Bernard, Bradford Jensen, and Peter Schott (*Journal of Monetary Economics*, 2006), industries experiencing "relatively large" reductions in costs associated with international trade exhibit strong productivity growth. Here, the authors consider costs of trade to be transportation costs and industry-level export and import tariffs.

Yet another study on the subject cautions against overly optimistic news, and finds that rosy estimates of the future impact of technology on productivity may cause boom-bust cycles in the longer term. The research by Lawrence Christiano, Cosmin Ilut, Roberto Motto, and Massimo Rostagno (European Central Bank, Working Paper Series 955), finds that because wages increase on productivity news but do not decrease on a lack of such news, productivity news that failed to materialize causes a discrepancy between the employees' costs and their performance, leading to larger market disruptions.

Overall, investors should follow the news on future productivity in estimating their projections for financial securities. While the productivity index delivers an assessment of whether expected productivity has materialized, it does not affect markets as much.

MONETARY AND FINANCIAL DATA

OCTOBER 2011

Sun	Mon	Tue	Wed	Thu	Fri	Sat
						1
2	3	4	5	6	7	8
9	10	11	12	13	14	15
16	17	18	19	20	21	22
23	24	25	26	27	28	29
30	31					

KEY HIGHLIGHTS

Monetary and financial data holds insights to future prosperity of the nation.

- Bank Stocks Shrink When Money Supply Is Tightened
- Flow of Funds Forecasts Economy in Medium Term
- Watch Out for Stealth Monetary Base Expansions before Elections
- Senior Loan Officers Have Insights into GDP Growth
- Consumer Credit is Welcomed by Retailers

OCTOBER

Bank Stocks Shrink When Money Supply Is Tightened

Expectations about the supply of money can have a material impact on trading. One of the statistics to monitor is the U.S. Money Supply. Money Supply measures money available in circulation, and is one of several variables, collectively known as Monetary Aggregates, reported by the U.S. Federal Reserve every Thursday at 4:30 P.M.

Monetary Aggregates encompass three groups of variables, known as M1, M2, M3, and L. M1 variables include currency in circulation (cash) and cash alternatives, such as travelers checks, deposits available on demand, and other financial instruments immediately transferable into cash. M2 variables include all M1 variables in addition to overnight bank lending, money market accounts, small savings accounts, and other short-term deposits. M3 variables include all of the above figures in addition to larger savings accounts and accounts with medium-term time lock-ups, such as term deposits. Finally, L figures include M3 and longer term deposits, like U.S. bonds.

Figure 28 shows the average response of the price of a bank stock, in this case Bank of America (BAC), to changes in the U.S. money supply. As

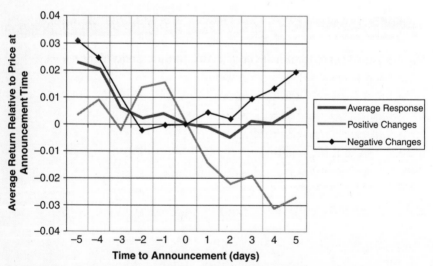

Figure 28   Response of BAC to Changes in the U.S. Money Supply.

Events this week:

- Pending Home Sales Index
- Challenger, Gray & Christmas Employment Report
- Unit Auto and Truck Sales for September 2011
- Manufacturers' Shipments, Inventories, and Orders for August 2011
- Job Opening and Labor Turnover Survey (JOLTS)

Monday, October 3, 2011

10:00 A.M.	ISM Report on Business—Manufacturing for September 2011
10:00 A.M.	Construction Spending for August 2011
11:00 A.M.	U.S. Treasury Bill Auction Announcement

Tuesday, October 4, 2011

7:45 A.M.	ICSC Retail Sales Index
8:55 A.M.	Johnson Redbook Report
5:00 P.M.	ABC News Consumer Comfort Index

Wednesday, October 5, 2011

7:00 A.M.	U.S. Mortgage Application Indexes
8:15 A.M.	ADP National Employment Report
10:00 A.M.	ISM Report on Business—Non-Manufacturing for September 2010

Thursday, October 6, 2011

6:00 A.M.	Monster Employment Index
7:00 A.M.	Bank of England Rate Decision (U.K.)
7:45 A.M.	European Central Bank Interest Rate Announcement
8:30 A.M.	U.S. Unemployment Insurance Claims
11:00 A.M.	13- and 26-Week U.S. T-Bill Auction Announcements
4:30 P.M.	U.S. Monetary Aggregates
4:30 P.M.	U.S. Monetary Base

Friday, October 7, 2011

8:30 A.M.	The Employment Situation

Notes: _____

OCTOBER

Figure 28 (on page 130) shows, when money supply increases, the stock price of the bank tends to fall; whereas when the money price decreases, the BAC stock price rises.

This curious reaction is likely related to the fact that an increase in the supply of money tends to be accompanied by higher inflation, whereby the price of the same product rises from one year to the next simply due to the increases of money in circulation (assuming the number of products available for sale stays constant). One of the main businesses of banks is lending. To lend money profitably, banks need to charge an interest rate that is above inflation. If a bank lends money out at a fixed rate (as it does when issuing mortgages), and there is significant inflation, the bank is at risk of losing money. Therefore, when money supply increases, bank stocks decline to reflect the possibility that they may experience losses on their fixed-rate loans.

To trade banking stocks on money supply announcements, quant investors can buy banking stocks when the money supply is announced as decreasing, and sell banking stocks when money supply increases.

Flow of Funds Forecasts Economy in Medium Term

Since 1952, the U.S. Federal Reserve has published details about the aggregate balance sheet of households, businesses, federal, state, and local governments. The data tracks flows of assets and debt in the economy, including:

- Financial institutions' sources of borrowing and lending
- U.S. households' distribution of assets among common deposit and investment funds
- The relative level of indebtedness of individuals, known as the savings rate
- The financing gaps of corporations compares operating cash flows with investments into capital, inventory accumulation and ultimately the flows of debt/dividends
- Household investments into residential real estate

From an investor's perspective, the flow of funds report shows an interesting statistic related to housing that helps predict the health

OCTOBER 10–16, 2011

Events this week:

- U.S. NFIB Small Business Optimism Index for September 2011
- U.S. Industrial Production and Capacity Utilization for September 2011
- U.S. Manufacturing and Trade Inventories and Sales for August 2011
- U.S. Retail Sales for September 2011
- Manufacturers' Shipments, Inventories, and Orders for August 2011
- International Trade Balance for August 2011
- Treasury International Capital Flows for August 2011
- Job Opening and Labor Turnover Survey (JOLTS)
- Consumer Price Index
- Producer Price Index
- Productivity and Costs
- Import and Export Prices

Monday, October 10, 2011

Columbus Day (U.S. Markets Closed)

Sports Day (Japan Markets Closed)

Tuesday, October 11, 2011

- 7:45 A.M.   ICSC Retail Sales Index
- 8:55 A.M.   Johnson Redbook Report
- 5:00 P.M.   ABC News Consumer Comfort Index

Wednesday, October 12, 2011

- 7:00 A.M.   U.S. Mortgage Application Indexes
- 2:00 P.M.   U.S. Federal Budget Balance

Thursday, October 13, 2011

Canadian Thanksgiving (Canadian Markets Closed)

- 8:30 A.M.   U.S. Unemployment Insurance Claims
- 11:00 A.M.   13- and 26-Week U.S. T-Bill Auction Announcements
- 4:30 P.M.   U.S. Monetary Aggregates
- 4:30 P.M.   U.S. Monetary Base

Friday, October 14, 2011

- 10:00 A.M.   U.S. Consumer Sentiment, preliminary data

Notes:

OCTOBER

of the U.S. economy in the medium term. In particular, household inflows into residential real estate indicate rising housing markets. According to the research of John D. Benjamin, Peter Chinloy, and G. Donald Jud (*Journal of Real Estate Finance and Economics*, 2004), when the value of people's real estate holdings rise, individual consumers feel much wealthier. As a result, consumers are likely to spend more when their real estate increases in value. The increase in consumer spending, in turn, propels the economy.

Specifically, Benjamin, Chinloy, and Jud estimate that for every additional dollar increase in their real estate wealth, consumers increase their spending by eight cents in the same year. By comparison, for every additional dollar increase in their investment portfolio wealth, consumers increase their spending by only two cents over the same year. The higher the consumer spending, the better is the economic state of the nation, and vice versa. Declines in stock markets typically cause decreases in consumer spending, and can trigger a recession. However, declines in real estate values may have a much more profound negative impact on consumer spending, and may even freeze the economy.

As a result, positive changes in inflows into residential real estate may forecast the medium-term state of the economy. The higher the inflows are, the higher the probability that the economy will thrive through the year.

WATCH OUT FOR STEALTH MONETARY BASE EXPANSIONS BEFORE ELECTIONS

The monetary base measures the supply of money readily used by the banking system for lending. To measure this lending potential, or "leverage," of the U.S. banking system, the U.S. Federal Reserve Board tracks the following parameters:

- Total bank reserves
- Currencies in circulation
- Cash held by banks

Increases in the monetary base often lead to a temporary increase in economic activity. This improvement often comes at a price in the form of increases in the aggregate money base, ultimately resulting in inflation.

OCTOBER 17–23, 2011

Events this week:

- U.S. Durable Goods Orders for September 2011
- Bank of Canada Target Bank Rate Announcement
- Composite Index of Leading Economic Indicators for September 2011
- U.S. Retail Sales for September 2011
- Housing Starts and Building Permits for September 2011
- Treasury International Capital Flows for August 2011
- Consumer Price Index

Monday, October 17, 2011

8:30 A.M.	Empire State Manufacturing Survey
11:00 A.M.	U.S. Treasury Bill Auction Announcement

Tuesday, October 18, 2011

7:45 A.M.	ICSC Retail Sales Index
8:55 A.M.	Johnson Redbook Report
5:00 P.M.	ABC News Consumer Comfort Index

Wednesday, October 19, 2011

7:00 A.M.	U.S. Mortgage Application Indexes
7:00 A.M.	Bank of England Minutes of the Monetary Policy Committee (U.K.)
2:00 P.M.	Current Economic Conditions ("Beige Book")

Thursday, October 20, 2011

8:30 A.M.	U.S. Unemployment Insurance Claims
10:00 A.M.	Philadelphia Fed Business Outlook Survey
11:00 A.M.	13- and 26-Week U.S. T-Bill Auction Announcements
4:30 P.M.	U.S. Monetary Aggregates
4:30 P.M.	U.S. Monetary Base

Friday, October 21, 2011

12:00 P.M.	October 2011 option expiration

Notes:

OCTOBER

According to a large body of macroeconomic research, an incumbent governments with medium to poor reelection prospects are particularly likely to expand the monetary base ahead of elections, with the hope that the temporary spike in economic activity prompts their reelection. After the election, the monetary base is contracted, inflationary expectations are reduced, and the status quo rolls on.

All else held equal, a sudden expansion in the monetary base is likely to cause a devaluation in foreign exchange, a highly noticeable reaction likely to receive criticism from the government's constituents. According to the latest research of Axel Dreher and Roland Vaubel (*Journal of International Money and Finance*, 2009), governments hide their surprise pre-election monetary expansions by stabilizing foreign exchange through open-market operations.

Using 1975–2001 data for 146 countries, Dreher and Vaubel show that pre-election spending is deployed by governments around the world. Furthermore, governments hide their pre-election monetary activities by selling large amounts of foreign exchange out of government reserves in the open markets.

While such operations leave little obvious traces, investors should be aware of sudden economic upticks ahead of elections. These bursts of economic activity may just be monetary window-dressing.

SENIOR LOAN OFFICERS HAVE INSIGHTS INTO GDP GROWTH

Since 1966, the U.S. Federal Reserve has been polling senior loan officers at large U.S. banks to keep track of lending practices and their outlook. The Senior Loan Officers' survey is conducted quarterly and includes questions on current and projected demand for loans from households and businesses. According to the 2006 research of Thomas Cunningham from the Federal Reserve Bank of Atlanta, the survey seldom yields accurate predictions of the banking sector's future. Yet surprisingly, the survey correctly forecasts future growth in Gross Domestic Product (GDP) as much as two quarters ahead.

Events this week:

- Advance GDP Figures, third quarter 2011, U.S.
- Advance Personal Income, third quarter 2011, U.S.
- U.S. Housing Vacancies and Home Ownership Rates
- U.S. Durable Goods Orders for September 2011
- Bank of Canada Target Bank Rate Announcement
- Manufacturers' Shipments, Inventories, and Orders for September 2011
- Personal Consumption Expenditures for September 2011
- PCE- and GDP-Based Price Indexes for September 2011
- Employment Cost Index for third quarter 2011

Monday, October 24, 2011

11:00 A.M.	U.S. Treasury Bill Auction Announcement

Tuesday, October 25, 2011

7:45 A.M.	ICSC Retail Sales Index
8:55 A.M.	Johnson Redbook Report
9:00 A.M.	S&P/Case-Shiller Home Price Indexes September 2011
10:00 A.M.	Richmond Federal Reserve Bank Survey for September 2011
10:00 A.M.	Consumer Confidence
10:00 A.M.	Existing Home Sales for September 2011
5:00 P.M.	ABC News Consumer Comfort Index

Wednesday, October 26, 2011

7:00 A.M.	U.S. Mortgage Application Indexes

Thursday, October 27, 2011

8:30 A.M.	U.S. Unemployment Insurance Claims
10:00 A.M.	Help Wanted Advertising Index for September 2011
11:00 A.M.	Kansas City Federal Reserve Bank Manufacturing Survey for September 2011
11:00 A.M.	13- and 26-Week U.S. T-Bill Auction Announcements
4:30 P.M.	U.S. Monetary Aggregates
4:30 P.M.	U.S. Monetary Base

Friday, October 28, 2011

10:00 A.M.	U.S. Consumer Sentiment, preliminary data

Notes:

OCTOBER

Table 8   Key Questions and Movement of GDP

Question	Growth in Real GDP
Increased willingness to make consumer loans	+
Tightening standards for commercial and industrial loans to large and medium firms	−
Tightening standards for commercial and industrial loans to small firms	−
Increasing spread for commercial and industrial loans to large and medium firms	−
Increasing spread for commercial and industrial loans to small firms	−

The survey queries loan officers on their willingness to make consumer installment loans, commercial and industrial loans to small, medium, and large firms, and whether loan officers have witnessed an increase in loan spreads, to name a few categories. Only five possible answers are allowed: "more," "much more," "less," "much less," or "about the same."

Cunningham identifies the following questions from the survey (see Table 8), positive responses to which have correctly predicted various macroeconomic variables. Registering a highly positive or highly negative response to a question in the latest survey helps investors to forecast GDP movement over the following two quarters.

The key questions and the subsequent movements of GDP are summarized in Table 8. A "+" in the right-hand column indicates that a highly positive response to the question is followed by a growth in real GDP, whereas a "−" in the right-hand column indicates a decline in GDP in response to a positive response to the question. Thus, if "willingness to make consumer loans" is reported to have increased markedly, the U.S. GDP may be growing over the following two quarters.

CONSUMER CREDIT IS WELCOMED
BY RETAILERS

The monthly Consumer Credit report, produced by the U.S. Federal Reserve Board, comprises the amount of short-term consumer credit outstanding by the previous month's end.

OCTOBER 31–NOVEMBER 6, 2011

Events this week:

- Advance GDP Figures, third quarter 2011, U.S.
- Advance Personal Income, third quarter 2011, U.S.
- Manufacturers' Shipments, Inventories, and Orders for September 2011
- U.S. Housing Vacancies and Homeownership Rates
- PCE- and GDP-Based Price Indexes for September 2011
- Employment Cost Index for third quarter 2011

Monday, October 31, 2011

9:45 A.M.   Chicago Business Barometer

11:00 A.M.   U.S. Treasury Bill Auction Announcement

Notes: _____

OCT/NOV

In the report, outstanding consumer credit is listed by issuer and type of credit. Issuers are broken down into these classifications.

- Commercial banks
- Finance companies
- Credit unions
- Federal government
- Savings institutions
- Nonfinancial business
- Pools of securitized assets

All credit is further categorized into revolving and nonrevolving credit. Revolving credit includes credit cards, credit lines, and any other type of credit that individuals can use to make any purchases. Nonrevolving credit refers to purchase-specific lending that is not available for general use. A mortgage is an example of nonrevolving credit, good only for purchase of one property.

Higher consumer credit is a boon to retailers. Figure 29 shows the average response of retailer Home Depot (ticker: HD) to changes in consumer credit. Positive responses trigger rises in the stock price of HD.

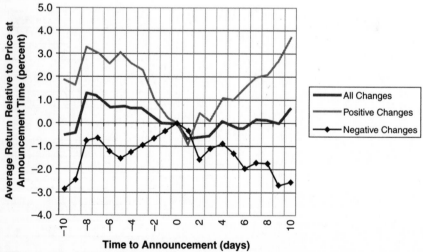

Figure 29   Response of HD to Changes in the U.S. Consumer Credit.

FEDERAL RESERVE POLICY AND FEDERAL GOVERNMENT FINANCES

NOVEMBER 2011

Sun	Mon	Tue	Wed	Thu	Fri	Sat
		1	2	3	4	5
6	7	8	9	10	11	12
13	14	15	16	17	18	19
20	21	22	23	24	25	26
27	28	29	30			

KEY HIGHLIGHTS

This month we examine selected aspects of the Federal Reserve policy.

- U.S. Treasury Bill Offerings on Foreign Exchange
- Federal Reserve Bank Credit on the Markets
- Is There a Floor for U.S. Interest Rates?
- Interest Rates Around the World
- Distilling Upcoming Interest Rate Possibilities from Market Data

NOVEMBER

U.S. TREASURY BILL OFFERINGS ON FOREIGN EXCHANGE

To fund spending and to make payments on outstanding debt, the U.S. Department of Treasury issues four types of securities: Treasury Bills (T-Bills), Treasury notes, Treasury bonds, and Treasury Inflation Protected Securities (TIPS). All Treasury-issued securities have bond-like structures, yet they have different maturity dates and interest rates.

- T-Bills mature within one year and pay no interest until maturity.
- Treasury notes mature in 2 to 10 years, and pay a predetermined coupon rate every 6 months.
- Treasury bonds mature in 20 to 30 years and also pay a semiannual coupon.
- TIPS are inflation-indexed bonds that have a semiannual coupon, yet whose nominal amount, or principal, grows along with the inflation rate.

T-Bills with maturities of 4, 13, and 26 weeks are offered for sale every week. The number of T-Bills offered for sale at any given time cannot exceed

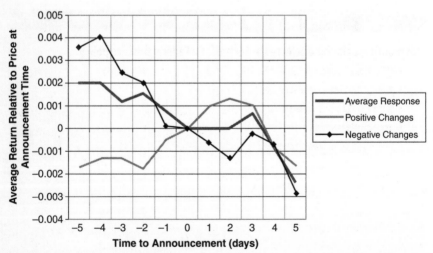

Figure 30   Response of GBP/USD to Changes in the U.S. Four-Week T-Bill Offering Amount.

Events this week:

- Advance GDP Figures, third quarter 2011, U.S.
- Advance Personal Income, third quarter 2011, U.S.
- Pending Home Sales Index
- Challenger, Gray & Christmas Employment Report
- Unit Auto and Truck Sales for October 2011
- Manufacturers' Shipments, Inventories, and Orders for September 2011
- Job Opening and Labor Turnover Survey (JOLTS)

Tuesday, November 1, 2011

🛒	7:45 A.M.	ICSC Retail Sales Index
🛒	8:55 A.M.	Johnson Redbook Report
⊕	10:00 A.M.	ISM Report on Business—Manufacturing for October 2011
🏠	10:00 A.M.	Construction Spending for September 2011
🛒	5:00 P.M.	ABC News Consumer Comfort Index

Wednesday, November 2, 2011

🏠	7:00 A.M.	U.S. Mortgage Application Indexes
💼	8:15 A.M.	ADP National Employment Report

Thursday, November 3, 2011

Culture Day (Japan Markets Closed)

💼	6:00 A.M.	Monster Employment Index
💰	7:45 A.M.	European Central Bank Interest Rate Announcement
💼	8:30 A.M.	U.S. Unemployment Insurance Claims
⊕	10:00 A.M.	ISM Report on Business—Non-Manufacturing for October 2010
🏠	10:00 A.M.	OFHEO Home Price Index, U.S.
💰	11:00 A.M.	13- and 26-Week U.S. T-Bill Auction Announcements
📈	4:30 P.M.	U.S. Monetary Aggregates
📈	4:30 P.M.	U.S. Monetary Base

Friday, November 4, 2011

💼	8:30 A.M.	The Employment Situation

Notes:

the limits set by the U.S. Congress, yet varies according to internal decisions made by the Treasury based on the short-term financial situation of
the U.S. government.

Increases in the size of T-Bill offerings raise fears of increased budget
deficits and a weaker U.S. dollar. Figure 30 (on page 142) illustrates the
impact of week-to-week changes in the 4-week T-Bill on the British Pound
Sterling/U.S. Dollar (GDP/USD) exchange rate. When the supply of T-bills
increases from one week to the next, the British pound rises relative to the
U.S. dollar (the U.S. dollar weakens). Similarly, if it decreases from one week
to the next, the British pound strengthens relative to the U.S. dollar.

FEDERAL RESERVE BANK CREDIT ON
THE MARKETS

The Federal Budget Balance is the balance between federal receipts and
outlays. The balance is reported on a monthly basis and provides insights
into how the government is collecting and spending taxpayer money, as
well as how the government is financing its deficits.

One of the important sections in the Federal Budget Balance is the Credit
of the Federal Reserve Bank. The Credit is derived from three sources.

- Federal Reserve advances and discounts at the Federal Discount
  Window, a short-term safety valve for financial institutions in crisis.
- Longer-term Fed credits extended to financial institutions having
  liquidity problems.
- Treasury and other federal agency securities purchased by the Federal
  Reserve in open market operations.

Weekly changes in the Federal Reserve Bank Credit indicate trends in
the health of U.S. financial markets and U.S. inflation. The Credit is often
extended through newly printed money.

Figure 31 (on page 146) shows response of the U.S. Coca-Cola stock
(ticker: COKE) to weekly changes in the Reserve Bank Credit portion of
the Federal Balance Sheet. When the Reserve Bank Credit increases, COKE
sharply drops, and vice versa. This response is similar to, yet more pronounced, than COKE's response to announcements of realized inflation.

Events this week:

- U.S. NFIB Small Business Optimism Index for October 2011
- U.S. Manufacturing and Trade Inventories and Sales for September 2011
- International Trade Balance for September 2011
- Job Opening and Labor Turnover Survey (JOLTS)
- Productivity and Costs
- Import and Export Prices

Monday, November 7, 2011

11:00 A.M. U.S. Treasury Bill Auction Announcement

Tuesday, November 8, 2011

7:45 A.M. ICSC Retail Sales Index

8:55 A.M. Johnson Redbook Report

5:00 P.M. ABC News Consumer Comfort Index

Wednesday, November 9, 2011

7:00 A.M. U.S. Mortgage Application Indexes

Thursday, November 10, 2011

7:00 A.M. Bank of England Rate Decision (U.K.)

8:30 A.M. U.S. Unemployment Insurance Claims

11:00 A.M. 13- and 26-Week U.S. T-Bill Auction Announcements

2:00 P.M. U.S. Federal Budget Balance

4:30 P.M. U.S. Monetary Aggregates

4:30 P.M. U.S. Monetary Base

Friday, November 11, 2011

Veteran's Day (U.S. Markets Closed)

Notes:

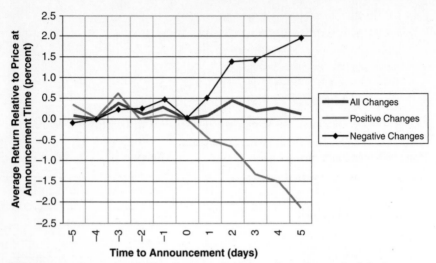

Figure 31   Response of COKE to Changes in Fed Balance Sheet, Reserve Bank Credit (United States).

IS THERE A FLOOR FOR U.S. INTEREST RATES?

Over the last few years, the U.S. has enjoyed historically low interest rates (Figure 32 on page 148 illustrates the trends). Rates are determined by the U.S. Federal Open Market Committee (FOMC) at the Federal Reserve. In the FOMC minutes released on March 16, 2010, the Committee members indicated their intent to keep rates low for an "extended period" of time. Yet, the natural question on the minds of many quantitative investors is can such low rates be sustained for a long time?

The Fed influences rates through "open market operations." This phrase is often mentioned in the minutes of the Fed and it refers to selectively buying and selling U.S. Treasury-issued securities with different maturities. The treasuries with different maturities carry different amounts of risk, have different liquidity, and are therefore viewed by investors as different financial products. The U.S. Fed is then able to influence the premiums investors are willing to pay for each Treasury-issued security by changing the supply and demand of these securities. For example, by buying 4-week U.S. T-Bills on

Events this week:

- U.S. Industrial Production and Capacity Utilization for October 2011
- U.S. Retail Sales for October 2011
- Composite Index of Leading Economic Indicators for October 2011
- Housing Starts and Building Permits for October 2011
- Treasury International Capital Flows for September 2011
- Consumer Price Index
- Producer Price Index
- Productivity and Costs

Monday, November 14, 2011

	11:00 A.M.	U.S. Treasury Bill Auction Announcement

Tuesday, November 15, 2011

	7:45 A.M.	ICSC Retail Sales Index
	8:30 A.M.	Empire State Manufacturing Survey
	8:55 A.M.	Johnson Redbook Report
	5:00 P.M.	ABC News Consumer Comfort Index

Wednesday, November 16, 2011

	7:00 A.M.	U.S. Mortgage Application Indexes
	7:00 A.M.	Bank of England Inflation Report (U.K.)

Thursday, November 17, 2011

	8:30 A.M.	U.S. Unemployment Insurance Claims
	10:00 A.M.	Philadelphia Fed Business Outlook Survey
	11:00 A.M.	13- and 26-Week U.S. T-Bill Auction Announcements
	4:30 P.M.	U.S. Monetary Aggregates
	4:30 P.M.	U.S. Monetary Base

Friday, November 18, 2011

	10:00 A.M.	U.S. Consumer Sentiment, preliminary data
	12:00 P.M.	November 2011 option expiration

Notes: _____

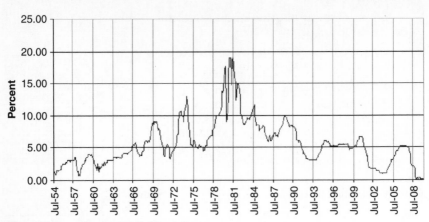

Figure 32   Effective U.S. Fed Funds Rate.

the open markets, the Fed reduces the supply of the 4-week T-Bills available to other investors, driving up prices. Since the price and yield of bonds are inversely related, once the price of the T-Bills rises, their yield falls. The banks respond to the new lower yields by lowering the rates at which they lend to each other, reducing the overall lending rates in the economy.

In a 2004 article, the current Federal Open Market Committee Chairman, Ben Bernanke, and Vincent R. Reinhart (*American Economic Review*) argue that a "quantitative easing" strategy enables governments to maintain very low interest rates for extended periods of time. The quantitative easing amounts to increasing the Fed balance sheet: It raises the amount of money the Fed has at its disposal to buy and sell Treasury securities. As long as the U.S. government has the capability to expand the Fed's balance sheet, U.S. interest rates may remain at their record lows.

INTEREST RATES AROUND THE WORLD

Many central banks around the world have adopted monetary policy processes similar to those of the Federal Open Markets Committee (FOMC) at the U.S. Fed. The designated interest rate committee members

Events this week:

- U.S. Durable Goods Orders for October 2011
- Personal Consumption Expenditures for October 2011

Monday, November 21, 2011

11:00 A.M.   U.S. Treasury Bill Auction Announcement

Tuesday, November 22, 2011

7:45 A.M.   ICSC Retail Sales Index

8:55 A.M.   Johnson Redbook Report

10:00 A.M.   Richmond Federal Reserve Bank Survey for October 2011

5:00 P.M.   ABC News Consumer Comfort Index

Wednesday, November 23, 2011

Labor Thanksgiving Day (Japan Markets Holiday)

7:00 A.M.   U.S. Mortgage Application Indexes

7:00 A.M.   Bank of England Minutes of the Monetary Policy
Committee (U.K.)

11:00 A.M.   Kansas City Federal Reserve Bank Manufacturing
Survey for October 2011

Thursday, November 24, 2011

U.S. Thanksgiving Day (U.S. Markets Closed)

Friday, November 25, 2011

10:00 A.M.   U.S. Consumer Sentiment, final data

10:00 A.M.   Existing Home Sales for October 2011

Notes:

NOVEMBER

independently consider various facets of economic activity, then meet on a designated date, discuss their views, vote for or against an interest rate change, and thus arrive at a decision to raise or lower their country's interest rates.

In Canada, the equivalent of the Fed Funds rate is known as the Target Bank Rate. In Britain, it is British Interest Rates that are decided upon by the Monetary Policy Committee (MPC) of the Bank of England. In the European Union, the key interest rates are determined by the Governing Council of the European Central Bank (ECB).

As with the United States, interest rates in each country significantly influence economic growth as well as prices of equities, foreign exchange, and other financial securities. To contain rumors and premature information ahead of the meetings that may cause undue volatility in the financial markets, interest rate committees impose embargoes on all communication prior to the official release of the committee decision and minutes.

Although many countries have adopted rate setting processes that appear similar, persistent differences exist. For example, according to Michael Ehrmann and Marcel Fratzscher (*Journal of Money Credit and Banking*, 2007), most of the interest-rate decisions by the U.S. FOMC are reached unanimously, while most of those by the MPC in England are not. Specifically, between May 1999 and May 2004, only 15 percent of the U.S. FOMC meetings ended without complete unanimity. In comparison, in England more than 54 percent of meetings end up with at least one dissenter. The exact voting distribution of committee members is released along with the meeting minutes, usually a few weeks following the interest rate decision announcement.

When committee members dissent, are there negative implications? According to Ehrmann and Fratzscher, more uniform decision voting, akin to that of the U.S. FOMC, leads to more predictable interest rate announcements. Predictable interest rate decisions are more quickly integrated into market prices and lower market volatility at the time these decisions are announced. The tradition of dissent in the U.K. generates a higher uncertainty in the markets ahead of interest rate announcements. Ultimately, each country's markets adapt to their central banks' idiosyncratic styles and manage the volatility. For example, higher volatility surrounding the U.K. announcements is great for going long options on U.K.-based equities just ahead of the announcements.

Events this week:

- Preliminary GDP Figures, third quarter 2011, U.S.
- Preliminary Personal Income, third quarter 2011, U.S.
- Preliminary Corporate Profits, third quarter 2011, U.S.
- Bank of Canada Target Bank Rate Announcement
- Manufacturers' Shipments, Inventories, and Orders for October 2011
- U.S. Durable Goods Orders for October 2011
- Housing Vacancies and Homeownership Rates
- PCE- and GDP-Based Price Indexes for October 2011

Monday, November 28, 2011

11:00 A.M.   U.S. Treasury Bill Auction Announcement

Tuesday, November 29, 2011

7:45 A.M.   ICSC Retail Sales Index

8:55 A.M.   Johnson Redbook Report

9:00 A.M.   S&P/Case-Shiller Home Price Indexes for October 2011

10:00 A.M.   Consumer Confidence

5:00 P.M.   ABC News Consumer Comfort Index

Wednesday, November 30, 2011

7:00 A.M.   U.S. Mortgage Application Indexes

8:15 A.M.   ADP National Employment Report

9:45 A.M.   Chicago Business Barometer

Notes: _____

DISTILLING UPCOMING INTEREST RATE POSSIBILITIES FROM MARKET DATA

The anticipation of federal interest rate decisions by central banks creates uncertainty about the direction of the economy. Yet, according to William Emmons, Aeimit Lakdawala, and Christopher Neely (Federal Reserve Bank of St. Louis, 2006), this uncertainty can be successfully harnessed to predict the announcement ahead of time and to profitably trade on it.

The key to these authors' argument is that the uncertainty preceding central bank decisions on key interest rates, and traders' opinions on the likelihood of one decision outcome or another, is reflected in the markets. In the United States, the nearest-expiration futures on the federal fund rates reflect market point forecast of the rates.

The point forecast, however, may be unreliable if it is generated by highly dispersed opinions of traders. One way to estimate the dispersion of views is by observing the volatility of the nearest-expiration futures contracts on the federal fund rates. The wider the dispersion of views on the outcome of the upcoming announcement, the higher the futures' volatility.

Another way to measure the cohesiveness of market opinion on the outcome of the announcement is to observe the pricing of options on the nearest expiration futures on Fed funds rate. Take two options with the same nearest-term futures contract. If the options are identical in every respect except their strike prices, then the difference in the prices of the options reflects the difference in probability that the options will end up "in the money," i.e., that the strike price of options is in the right ballpark. The wider the difference in prices of the two options, the higher the probability that the more expensive option reflects the interest rate decision anticipated by the markets. On the other hand, the lower the spread of options identical in every respect except their strike prices, the higher the underlying dispersion of the market opinions on the upcoming announcement.

Using options to build intuition about the uncertainty of upcoming announcements allows investors to hone their forecasts of interest rates and try to anticipate market reactions in other instruments following interest rate announcements. The low-dispersion forecasts are highly probable and can be used with a greater degree of confidence.

INNOVATIVE TRADING IDEAS

DECEMBER 2011

Sun	Mon	Tue	Wed	Thu	Fri	Sat
				1	2	3
4	5	6	7	8	9	10
11	12	13	14	15	16	17
18	19	20	21	22	23	24
25	26	27	28	29	30	31

KEY HIGHLIGHTS

Let's end the year with a preview of some topics we'll be examining in the 2012 Almanac.

- High-Frequency Trading
- Can the Momentum of Some Stocks Predict the Direction of Others?
- Trading on Option Expiration
- Stocks That Rose Last December Are Likely to Rise This December, Too
- The Monday Effect

HIGH-FREQUENCY TRADING

High-frequency trading (HFT) uses computer programs, known as algorithms, to hold short-term positions in equities, options, futures, ETFs, currencies, or any security that has adopted electronic trading. (Some securities, like credit default swaps, for example, cannot be traded electronically and are incompatible with investment algorithms.)

Aiming to capture just a fraction of a penny per share or currency unit on every trade, high-frequency traders move in and out of such short-term positions several times each day. Fractions of a penny accumulate fast to produce significantly positive results at the end of every day.

High-frequency trading became a buzzword in 2009, when Goldman Sachs accused one of their former employees of stealing their "cash cow," a sophisticated computer program capable of generating millions of dollars in trading profits over short periods of time. Yet, HFT has been around since the early 1980s, when several stock exchanges first decided to experiment with electronic trading. Since the 1980s, HFT has been growing in scope, speed, and complexity.

At the heart of HFT is the simple idea that properly programmed computers are better traders than humans. Computers can easily read and process amounts of data so large that it is inconceivable to humans. For example, frequently traded financial securities such as the EUR/USD exchange rate can produce well over 100 distinct quotes each second. Each quote, or "tick," carries unique information about concurrent market conditions. And while a dedicated team of human traders may be able to detect some tradable irregularities, the flow of trades has grown to the point that human brains are now no match for computers that can accurately resolve and act upon all the information entering the markets every moment. Add to that the fact that computers seldom get ill, are easily replaceable, and have no emotions. Oh, and they've become really cheap.

The complexity of computer technology now required by many HFT systems pales in comparison with modern video games. As video game purveyors drive the prices of advanced computer technology down, high-frequency trading becomes increasingly affordable to anyone with an inclination for quantitative analysis and programming. Call this a dot.com 4.0 revolution—the latest technology deployed in many other industries has finally arrived on Wall Street.

Events this week:

- Pending Home Sales Index
- Challenger, Gray & Christmas Employment Report
- Unit Auto and Truck Sales for November 2011
- ISM Semiannual Report
- Manufacturers' Shipments, Inventories, and Orders for October 2011
- Job Opening and Labor Turnover Survey (JOLTS)

Thursday, December 1, 2011

6:00 A.M. Monster Employment Index

8:30 A.M. U.S. Unemployment Insurance Claims

10:00 A.M. ISM Report on Business—Manufacturing for November 2011

10:00 A.M. Construction Spending for October 2011

11:00 A.M. 13- and 26-Week U.S. T-Bill Auction Announcements

4:30 P.M. U.S. Monetary Aggregates

Friday, December 2, 2011

8:30 P.M. The Employment Situation

Notes: _____

Some high-frequency trading strategies are quantitative investment strategies, like the ones in this book, deployed at high speeds. Other strategies that are specific to high-frequency trading, work with market minutiae, and they are known as "microstructure" strategies. In both cases, high-frequency traders feed off small intraday variations in prices and do not impact long-term investors.

Aldridge provides a comprehensive overview of high-frequency trading in her book, *High-Frequency Trading: A Practical Guide to Algorithmic Strategies and Trading Systems* (John Wiley & Sons, 2009).

CAN THE MOMENTUM OF SOME STOCKS PREDICT THE DIRECTION OF OTHERS?

Several academic studies have found that momentum in some stocks can predict the direction of other stocks. In other words, when one category ("Leader") of stocks rises or falls, another category ("Follower") follows suit in the same direction. Table 9 (on page 158) documents some of the leader-follower phenomena in the stock universe that have been identified in the academic literature to date.

TRADING ON OPTION EXPIRATION

The dates on which options expire are often considered to be a source of unwanted volatility in option prices, as well as prices of the underlying securities. However, recent research indicates that profitable strategies can be developed by observing the movement of the underlying security around the expiration date of its options.

First, a brief review of options. Options are rights, but not obligations, to buy or sell a share of a particular security at a specified price, known as the option's strike price, on or before the option expiration date. Options can be written on virtually any security. Options can be custom-made by an investment bank, and known as over-the-counter options (OTC). An increasingly large variety and volume of options are traded in fully standardized contracts on specialized options exchanges.

Events this week:

- ISM Semiannual Report
- Manufacturers' Shipments, Inventories, and Orders for October 2011
- International Trade Balance for October 2011
- Challenger, Gray & Christmas Employment Report
- Job Opening and Labor Turnover Survey (JOLTS)
- Flow of Funds

Monday, December 5, 2011

	10:00 A.M.	ISM Report on Business—Non-Manufacturing for November 2010
	11:00 A.M.	U.S. Treasury Bill Auction Announcement

Tuesday, December 6, 2011

	7:45 A.M.	ICSC Retail Sales Index
	8:55 A.M.	Johnson Redbook Report
	5:00 P.M.	ABC News Consumer Comfort Index

Wednesday, December 7, 2011

	7:00 A.M.	U.S. Mortgage Application Indexes
	2:00 P.M.	Current Economic Conditions ("Beige Book")

Thursday, December 8, 2011

	7:00 A.M.	Bank of England Rate Decision (U.K.)
	7:45 A.M.	European Central Bank Interest Rate Announcement
	8:30 A.M.	U.S. Unemployment Insurance Claims
	11:00 A.M.	13- and 26-Week U.S. T-Bill Auction Announcements
	4:30 P.M.	U.S. Monetary Aggregates
	4:30 P.M.	U.S. Monetary Base

Friday, December 9, 2011

Notes:

DECEMBER

Table 9   Leader-Follower Phenomena

Leaders	Followers	Key Finding	Authors of the Study
Stocks of customer firm	Stocks of supplier firm	When a customer of a supplier rises (declines), the supplier does too.	Lior Menzly and Oguzhan Ozbas (*Journal of Finance*, 2010)
Large stocks	Small stocks	Large stocks tend to lead small stocks	Lo, Andrew, and Craig MacKinlay (*Review of Financial Studies*, 1990)
Stocks in commercial real estate, petroleum, metal, retail, financial and services	The overall stock market and several economic indicators	Stocks in the leader industries are first to incorporate and reflect economic information	Harrison Hong, Walter Torous, and Rossen Valkanov (*Journal of Financial Economics*, 2007)
Stocks of firms covered by many equity analysts	Stocks of firms covered by few equity analysts	Equity analysts help impound information into stock prices	Michael Brennan, Narasimhan Jegadeesh, and Bhaskaran Swaminathan (*Review of Financial Studies*, 1993)
Stocks with high institutional ownership	Stocks with low institutional ownership	Stocks with large percentages owned by hedge funds and mutual funds lead stocks held mostly by individual investors	S. G. Badrinath, Jayant Kale, and Thomas Noe (*Review of Financial Studies*, 1995)

Standardized exchange-traded options have a set of peculiar features. Among them is what's called the discreteness of option strike prices: Strike prices of options tend to be spaced at regular intervals of at least one dollar. Thus, a stock trading at $21.67 may have outstanding option contracts with strikes of $20.00, $21.00, $22.00, and so on. In addition, most exchange-traded options expire on the third Friday of the month of their expiration. For example, an option expiring in June 2011 will actually expire on June 17, 2011.

DECEMBER 12–18, 2011

Events this week:

- U.S. NFIB Small Business Optimism Index for November 2011
- U.S. Industrial Production and Capacity Utilization for November 2011
- U.S. Manufacturing and Trade Inventories and Sales for October 2011
- U.S. Retail Sales for November 2011
- Composite Index of Leading Economic Indicators for November 2011
- Housing Starts and Building Permits for November 2011
- Current Account Balance, third quarter 2011
- Treasury International Capital Flows for October 2011
- Consumer Price Index
- Producer Price Index
- Productivity and Costs
- Import and Export Prices

Monday, December 12, 2011

11:00 A.M.	U.S. Treasury Bill Auction Announcement
2:00 P.M.	U.S. Federal Budget Balance

Tuesday, December 13, 2011

12:01 A.M.	Manpower Employment Outlook Survey
7:45 A.M.	ICSC Retail Sales Index
8:55 A.M.	Johnson Redbook Report
5:00 P.M.	ABC News Consumer Comfort Index

Wednesday, December 14, 2011

7:00 A.M.	U.S. Mortgage Application Indexes

Thursday, December 15, 2011

8:30 A.M.	Empire State Manufacturing Survey
8:30 A.M.	U.S. Unemployment Insurance Claims
10:00 A.M.	Philadelphia Fed Business Outlook Survey
11:00 A.M.	13- and 26-Week U.S. T-Bill Auction Announcements
4:30 P.M.	U.S. Monetary Aggregates
4:30 P.M.	U.S. Monetary Base

Friday, December 16, 2011

10:00 A.M.	U.S. Consumer Sentiment, preliminary data
12:00 P.M.	December 2011 option expiration

Notes: _____

Option expiration causes a discontinuity in option prices, as the option ceases to exist. Option contracts in the money at expiry will be exchanged for the underlying instrument, purchased at the strike price of the option. If the option is out of the money, the option is said to expire worthless, and the option buyer loses his option investment.

Interestingly, the effect of the option expiration date on prices does not stop at option prices. Several academic studies conducted over the years assessed the behavior of securities underlying the options, and concluded that option expiration also tends to affect prices of the underlying securities. As far as equities and equity options are concerned, Sophie Xiaoyan Ni, Neil D. Pearson, and Allen M. Poteshman, of the University of Illinois at Urbana-Champagne (*Journal of Financial Economics,* 2005), find that on expiration dates, prices of optionable equities cluster around the option strike prices. For example, a stock price that opens at $22.72 on an options expiry day is likely to gravitate to the nearest strike price by the end of the day, in this case, $23.00. To realize a profit in our example, an investor would buy shares of this security shortly after the open on the option expiration day and sell them at the close, realizing a gain of $0.28 per share. Understanding this behavior allows investors to capture intraday gains on underlying equities on the day their options expire.

STOCKS THAT ROSE LAST DECEMBER ARE LIKELY TO RISE THIS DECEMBER, TOO

Recent academic research shows that over the last 20 years stocks have followed seasonal monthly patterns. A stock that rose last December is likely to rise again this December.

Professors Steven L. Heston of the Kellogg School of Management and Ronie Sadka of Boston College (*Journal of Financial and Quantitative Analysis,* forthcoming) attribute this phenomenon to seasonal variation in stock returns. In addition to seasonality in stock returns, Heston and Sadka find that trading volume and intra-month volatility also show recurrent patterns: High-volume September in the last year is likely to lead to high-volume September this year; and low-volatility June of 2010 is likely to be followed by a low-volatility June in 2011.

DECEMBER 19–25, 2011

Events this week:

- U.S. Durable Goods Orders for November 2011
- Housing Starts and Building Permits for November 2011
- Existing Home Sales for November 2011

Monday, December 19, 2011

11:00 A.M.   U.S. Treasury Bill Auction Announcement

Tuesday, December 20, 2011

7:45 A.M.   ICSC Retail Sales Index

8:55 A.M.   Johnson Redbook Report

5:00 P.M.   ABC News Consumer Comfort Index

Wednesday, December 21, 2011

7:00 A.M.   U.S. Mortgage Application Indexes

7:00 A.M.   Bank of England Minutes of the Monetary Policy Committee (U.K.)

Thursday, December 22, 2011

8:30 A.M.   U.S. Unemployment Insurance Claims

11:00 A.M.   13- and 26-Week U.S. T-Bill Auction Announcements

4:30 P.M.   U.S. Monetary Aggregates

4:30 P.M.   U.S. Monetary Base

Friday, December 23, 2011

Emperor's Birthday (Japan Markets Holiday)

Notes:

DECEMBER

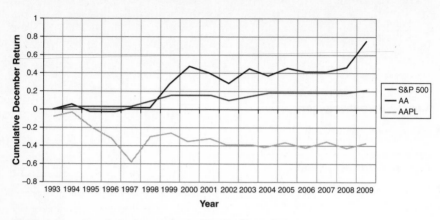

Figure 33   Cumulative Returns for the Month of December.

Trading on seasonality requires monthly portfolio rebalancing. At the end of each month, the portfolio is liquidated—all positions closed. At the beginning of each month, a portfolio is established again: Stocks that produced positive returns during the same month last year are bought, and stocks that lost value during the same month the previous year are sold. Heston and Sadka document that such trading strategies produce about 0.7 percent per month, gross of transaction costs. Investors carefully managing their transaction costs are able to capture consistent annual returns.

Figure 33 shows cumulative December returns for the S&P 500, Alcoa (AA), and Apple, Inc (AAPL). The December returns were computed as a percentage increase registered from the closing price on the last trading day of the preceding November to the closing price of the last trading day of December. As Figure 33 shows, S&P 500 and AA tend to rise in December, while AAPL stock tends to fall during the month.

THE MONDAY EFFECT

Stocks tend to generate larger returns on Fridays than on subsequent Mondays. This phenomenon is known as the Monday effect or the weekend effect, and has been observed by various researchers over the past three decades.

Events this week:

- Manufacturers' Shipments, Inventories, and Orders for November 2011
- Personal Consumption Expenditures for November 2011
- U.S. Durable Goods Orders for November 2011
- Existing Home Sales for November 2011
- PCE- and GDP-Based Price Indexes for November 2011

Monday, December 26, 2011

Christmas Observed (Financial Markets Closed in the Americas, Europe, and Japan)

Boxing Day (Markets closed in the U.K., Canada, Australia, New Zealand, and South Africa)

Tuesday, December 27, 2011

Markets Closed in the U.K., Canada, Australia, New Zealand, and South Africa (Christmas falls on a Sunday)

🛒	7:45 A.M.	ICSC Retail Sales Index
🛒	8:55 A.M.	Johnson Redbook Report
🏠	9:00 A.M.	S&P/Case-Shiller Home Price Indexes for November 2011
⊕	10:00 A.M.	Richmond Federal Reserve Bank Survey for November 2011
🛒	10:00 A.M.	Consumer Confidence
🛒	5:00 P.M.	ABC News Consumer Comfort Index

Wednesday, December 28, 2011

🏠	7:00 A.M.	U.S. Mortgage Application Indexes

Thursday, December 29, 2011

	6:00 A.M.	Monster Employment Index
💼	8:30 A.M.	U.S. Unemployment Insurance Claims
⊕	10:00 A.M.	ISM Report on Non-Manufacturing sectors
💼	10:00 A.M.	Help Wanted Advertising Index for November 2011
⊕	11:00 A.M.	Kansas City Federal Reserve Bank Manufacturing Survey for December 2011
💵	11:00 A.M.	13- and 26-Week U.S. T-Bill Auction Announcements
📈	4:30 P.M.	U.S. Monetary Aggregates
📈	4:30 P.M.	U.S. Monetary Base

Friday, December 30, 2011

⊕	9:45 A.M.	Chicago Business Barometer
🛒	10:00 A.M.	U.S. Consumer Sentiment, final data

Notes: _____

_____

_____

_____

_____

_____

_____

_____

_____

_____

_____

_____

_____

_____

_____

_____

_____

_____

_____

_____

_____

_____

_____

_____

_____

_____

_____

_____

_____

_____

_____

_____

_____

_____

_____

_____

The cause of the Monday effect is not clear. According to the Efficient Market Hypothesis (EMH) of finance, prices move in response to news. Friday markets aggregate news from Thursday night to the end of the trading day Friday. Monday markets incorporate the news that was released over the weekend, when the markets were closed, as well the news released on Monday. Since Monday trading absorbs potentially more news than the Friday session, the Monday session should see proportionally larger returns, according to the EMH.

Stocks of large firms incur the negative change in price between Friday nights and Monday mornings, before the markets open. Stocks of smaller firms tend to incur the bulk of the negative returns in the first 45 minutes of the Monday trading session. The effect also appears to be more pronounced in the last two weeks of each month than at the beginning of the month.

The Monday effect has been attributed to differences in trading patterns between institutional and individual investors. Institutional investors, such as mutual funds, hedge funds, and proprietary trading desks, trade evenly throughout the week. Individual investors, however, tend to increase their activity on Mondays, and appear to sell more than to buy following the weekend. The Monday effect has been waning over the years, particularly in large stocks favored by institutional investors. Yet, in small stocks traded mostly by small investors, the Monday effect has persisted.

Another explanation put forth for the Monday effect posits that the effect is caused by institutional short-sellers. These short-sellers buy stocks on Friday nights to close their positions in order to avoid the risk of unfavorable news affecting their portfolios over the weekend. Closing their positions lifts the market on Friday nights. The same short-sellers then reopen their short positions Monday mornings, exerting selling pressure on stocks, depressing the markets, and thus causing the Monday effect.

The Monday effect has been observed internationally. In addition to the U.S. markets, the effect has been documented in the U.K., Canadian, Swiss, and Greek markets, as well as in India, Philippines, South Korea, Taiwan, and Thailand.

GLOSSARY

active management An investment process; the investor or fund manager actively researches financial securities and updates his or her portfolios accordingly. Active management is the opposite of *passive management*.

algorithm A logical sequence of tasks, usually presented as a workflow that can be translated into a computer program.

algorithmic trading All trading that is facilitated by computer programs.

alpha A risk-adjusted return on investment, usually expressed as a percentage. Alpha is a return abstracted from broad market influences.

alternative investment A strategy that makes use of techniques other than long-only positions. Alternative investments include illiquid positions in the form of private equity and long-short strategies, like those deployed by hedge funds.

American option An option that can be exercised any time before expiration.

analyst report Investment analysis delivered by a professional security analyst.

arbitrage A strategy to trade away a temporary market disturbance.

Auto-Regressive Conditional Heteroscedasticity (ARCH) A model of evolution of financial data whereby future data and its variability are dependent on past data. ARCH and its close cousin Generalized ARCH (GARCH) are often used in financial modeling.

asset allocation A determination of which financial securities to select for investment.

asymmetric information A situation where one market participant has better information than another. Information asymmetry may be caused by several reasons: The better informed party may be more adept at research, or may subscribe to specialized paid-for research, among other factors.

at-the-money (ATM) A term used to describe near-par investments, usually options.

autocorrelation The degree to which past financial data of a particular security influences future financial data of the same security.

average annual return A return on a financial security, averaged over all the years since the security was first issued. For example, for a stock issued in 2007, the average annual return at the end of 2010 was the average of annual returns for 2007, 2008, 2009, and 2010.

back-test A process of applying a trading model to historic financial data in order to test a model's trading behavior. While a successful back-test does not guarantee that the model will work going forward, back-testing provides some degree of confidence that the model can perform, as well as an indication of risks embedded in the model.

bankruptcy Legal recognition of insolvency.

Bayesian Anything that makes educated guesses about the future based on historic outcomes. Bayesian decision-making processes continuously adjust probabilities of event occurrences based on the latest data.

bear market Recessions or similar economic environments characterized by prolonged absence of growth in the stock markets.

beta A measure of the market risk of an investment. Beta of 1 indicates that the investment carries a risk similar to that of the stock market. High beta characterizes investments with a higher risk relative to that of the market.

bid-ask spread A difference between the best bid and the ask quoted by brokers or exchanges at any given point in time. The bid-ask spread is a cost to investors; anyone buying and selling financial securities implicitly pays the bid-ask spread.

Black-Scholes An equation frequently used to price options.

bond A financial contract that usually pays a fixed semi-annual premium until the contract's "maturity" in exchange for an upfront investment, known as "principal." At maturity, the buyer of the bond receives the refund of the principal.

bondholder A buyer of a bond.

broker-dealer A financial market intermediary that buys and sells securities and charges a fee on each trade.

bull market Economic conditions characterized by persistent gains in stock markets.

buy-and-hold An investment strategy that involves buying ("going long") and holding securities, usually stocks, for prolonged periods of time.

call   An option that gives the buyer the right, but not the obligation, to buy a certain security ("the underlying") for a specified price ("the strike price"). The call typically expires on a prespecified date, known as the "expiration date."

capacity   The maximum amount that can be invested into a particular investment strategy before the strategy's returns begin to decline. The observed erosion of returns occurs when the market inefficiencies exploited by the strategy are fully exhausted.

capital   An amount of liquid assets available for investment.

Capital Asset Pricing Model (CAPM)   A famous financial model that stipulates that future return on a security is a function of the riskiness of the security and the future returns on financial markets as a whole.

capital gain (loss)   A gain (loss) on investments that were held for at least one full calendar year.

capital markets   Financial markets.

closing price   The last trade price observed on a particular trading day.

cloud computing   A network of computer systems distributing the programming workload over several processing engines, speeding up the computing operations.

cointegration   A statistical technique that detects dependencies of two variables. Unlike correlation, cointegration pinpoints cause-and-effect relationships.

collateral   An asset assigned as a trust item in a loan agreement. Should the borrower default on his loan obligation, the lender takes possession of the collateral.

colocation   A practice of placing computer processing power in locations near exchanges. Colocation saves on computer signal travel time.

commodity   A commonly used product traded as a financial security. Corn, oil, and even water are now commodities.

Commodity and Futures Trading Commission (CFTC)   A U.S. government organization regulating trading in commodities and futures.

comparable   A security whose properties are similar to those of another security.

contagion   A process whereby a movement of one security triggers similar movements in other securities.

convertible debt   Bonds that can be converted into corporate equity or other bonds at a prespecified time.

corporate bond   A loan borrowed by a corporation.

correlation   A measure of co-movement of any two variables.

coupon   A regular payment from the seller of the contract to the buyer of the contract. Coupons are common in bonds and similar financial instruments.

The term "coupon" harkens back to the era when bond contracts were printed on large sheets of paper with all coupons printed, similar to the layouts of modern supermarket leaflets. A bondholder desiring to obtain his coupon payment would clip the coupon, mail it in, and subsequently receive his coupon payment.

covariance   Another measure of co-movement of any two variables, this one amplified by variances of either variable.

credit rating   A score reflecting the ability of the borrower to repay his debt, known as creditworthiness. Credit ratings are assigned by credit rating agencies based on historical performance of the borrower, his current and past financials, and other often subjective characteristics.

credit spread   A difference in the market yield on a bond and a government T-Bill rate. Credit spreads accurately reflect the creditworthiness of the bond issuer, since all the market information about the issuer is impounded into the spread. Credit spreads are considered much better predictors of corporate credit worthiness than are ratings by bond rating companies, such as Moody's.

daily data   Security data sampled at daily intervals. Daily data typically includes daily open, high, low, close, and volume-traded information.

dark pools   Alternatives to exchanges where traders do not see information on other market participants, their positions, or their orders.

data points   A sequence of data, typically ordered by time stamp, used in quantitative analysis. Data points most often used in quantitative analysis include price, returns, trading volume, and volatility information.

data set   A collection of security-specific data points.

day order   A trading order that expires at the end of the day on which it was placed.

default   A financial condition indicating that the borrower failed to meet his loan obligations. A borrower is often considered to be in default when he fails to make payments for 90 calendar days past the payment due date. Default is not bankruptcy, which is a more complex legal judgment.

delivery   Physical delivery of goods or securities as specified in the trading contract. For example, future contracts have a delivery date on which the underlying goods or securities are delivered to the buyer of the futures. Commodities, such as corn, can be literally delivered to the futures buyer's doorstep. Securities, such as stocks or foreign exchange, are delivered to the futures buyer's trading account.

delta   A metric of by how much a derivative instrument moves when the price of the underlying security changes by $1.

demand   Quantities requested for purchase.

directional forecast   A forecast that indicates only a general direction (up or down) where the forecasted variable (price, volume, volatility, or other) is likely to move within a specified time frame. Unlike a point forecast, the directional forecast does not make predictions about the exact value of the forecasted variable.

directional trade   A bet that the traded security will rise within a forecasted time frame.

derivative   A security with payoff characteristics that are dependent upon the payoff characteristics of another security, called "the underlying."

distressed investing   Investing into "distressed" securities, the current owner or borrower of which is under pressure to sell.

distribution   A grouping of data points into "buckets," with each bucket containing data points corresponding to a certain value range. The objective of the grouping is to count the number of data points in each bucket in order to infer and compare the statistical frequency of data points in one range versus the other.

diversification   An investment methodology of spreading one's investments into multiple securities to mitigate investment risk.

dividend   A scheduled payment from a corporation to its shareholders. Dividends are typically a fraction of quarterly earnings of a corporation, set in advance by the corporate board.

drawdown   A cumulative loss of investment over a certain period of time during which the investment value failed to reach its high value before the loss.

econometrics   A branch of advanced statistics applied to economic and financial data.

electronic trading   All trading processed via computer networks.

emerging market   A financial market in a country with an economy undergoing rapid growth or industrialization.

equity   A stock; also capital invested.

error   A deviation from expectation.

European option   An option that can only be exercised on its expiration date.

event window   The time period before and after an economic "event," such as an earnings announcement or a macroeconomic news announcement. The event window is used to evaluate the impact of the event on securities. The window can be measured in seconds, hours, or months.

exchange fees   The fees charged by a securities exchange for matching one's trading order with another order posted on the exchange.

exchange-traded fund (ETF)   A mutual fund with shares traded on an exchange, side by side with the equity shares of corporations. Most ETFs tend to be passively managed. See *passive management.*

execution   Trade processing, typically handled by broker-dealers, exchanges, and inter-dealer networks.

expiration date   An end date of a financial contract; this term is primarily used in options and related contracts. The contract ceases to exist after it expires.

exponential   Nonlinear, typically fast-rising, relationship between two or more variables.

factor model   A model that attributes variation in data points of one security to variation in other "factors." The factors can be data of other securities, macro-economic news figures, and many other variables.

Federal Reserve (the Fed)   The central bank of the United States.

financial contract   A contractual agreement between the buyer and the seller of a financial instrument. The contract specifies the terms of the agreement.

financial instrument   A term that is used to describe a financial security: a stock, a bond, an option, a securitized mortgage obligation, among many others.

Federal Open Market Committee (FOMC)   A committee at the U.S. Federal Reserve that determines the target rate for the federal funds rate and oversees open market operations.

foreign exchange   A tradeable financial instrument that reflects the relative purchasing power differential in two countries. The purchasing power used in foreign exchange pricing is the relative ability to buy goods or financial securities, such as stocks and bonds.

fundamental analysis   A financial analysis that forecasts the future movement of securities based on projected corporate and industry growth, business models, economic outlook, and other "fundamental" information. Fundamental analysis may or may not be of a quantitative nature.

fund-of-funds   An investment vehicle whose specialty is the selection of mutual funds and hedge funds that are likely to be successful in the future. The fund-of-funds' managers make their investment selections on the basis of hedge fund track records, strategies, management credentials, and other relevant factors.

fund replication   A quantitative technique that allows an investor to mimic investment strategies of selected hedge funds. The technique involves identifying factors that drive the performance of selected hedge funds, using factor models. Once the factors driving the target hedge fund's performance are identified, the factors are used to put together an investment strategy mimicking the performance of the target funds.

futures   A tradeable financial contract that obliges the buyer to purchase a certain quantity of the underlying asset at a certain point in the future, known as the "delivery date." Popular futures contracts are written on corn, gold, crude oil, other commodities, foreign exchange, and individual equities. Many futures contracts are standardized in size and traded on specialized futures exchanges.

Global Tactical Asset Allocation (GTAA)   A quantitative portfolio allocation strategy that involves investing into financial securities and markets in different countries. When making their allocations, GTAA investors consider country growth, economic and political stability and risks, as well as relevant currency projections.

Good-Till-Cancel (GTC) Order   A trading order that is in force until the order is executed or the investor placing the order decides to cancel it. Some brokers automatically cancel GTC orders three months after they were placed.

hedge fund   A private investment partnership that allocates its clients' assets in any way other than the traditional buy-and-hold approach. Many hedge funds practice long-short equity strategies, where they are long some equities and short other equities, minimizing their cumulative market exposure.

hedging   An investing strategy designed to minimize the risk of the current investment portfolio composition.

heteroscedascicity   Time-varying volatility.

high-frequency trading   A set of computer-driven quantitative trading strategies with short position-holding periods and no overnight exposures.

high net worth   Investors with USD $1 million or more in investable assets.

high price   The highest price reached by a financial security during a given trading period.

high watermark   The highest net asset value the hedge fund achieved on record to date.

histogram   A graphical representation of a statistical *distribution.*

historical data   A set of historical security values. Historical data may include historical prices, returns, trading volume, volatility, or any other measurable financial characteristic. Historical data is typically organized in a *time series* format.

holding period   The time between when an investment portfolio position is opened and the time it is closed.

iceberg order   A trading order with only a small portion of the total order size displayed on the exchange.

index   A financial security that tracks the performance of a portfolio of several other financial securities.

inflation   A measure of increases in price levels.

initial public offering (IPO)   A process of selling a privately held company to the public. During an IPO in the United States, shares of a company are registered with the U.S. Securities and Exchange Commission (SEC). Following an IPO, the shares are traded on one or several U.S. exchanges.

in-sample Results of a *back-test* of a quantitative model performed on the sample of data on which the model was originally developed.

institutional Pertaining to a professional investment body, such as a pension fund, hedge fund, or mutual fund.

interest rate A compensation for time value of money; interest rates are paid by borrowers to lenders, and by money custodians (such as banks) to depositors.

internal rate of return The effective rate of return an investment generates throughout its lifetime.

in-the-money (ITM) Profitable; this term typically applies to option investments.

inventory The value of investments held by a firm. Outside of banking, inventory relates to the finished or partly finished products of corporations, or financial securities in the case of market-makers.

investing A process of analyzing markets, identifying likely scenarios, and placing one's capital behind the most probable strategies.

investing style A succinct description of one's beliefs and methods for making investment decisions.

investment banking A set of advisory activities for corporations that handles a wide range of tasks supporting investing. Investment banks do IPOs, make markets in various financial securities, and provide securities research and analysis, among other relevant activities.

issuer A corporation or a government issuing financial securities, such as stocks, bonds, and options.

kurtosis A measure of the likelihood of extreme events, such as highly negative returns.

leverage A loan an investor obtains with his capital as collateral. Leverage allows the investor to trade a multiple of his investment capital.

limit order A buy or sell order that specifies the desired execution price, in addition to other normal order characteristics.

linear Following a straight path. A linear relationship between any two variables means that, as one variable increases, another moves (increases or decreases) along a straight line in response.

liquidity The number of open orders on both buy (demand) and sell (supply) sides of a market.

liquidity pool A trading venue with open buy and sell orders.

liquidity risk The risk of being unable to find anyone to take the opposite side of a trade.

long A buy-and-hold investment strategy.

long-short An investment strategy that involves buying some financial securities and selling others in order to cancel out their common market risks.

lot size A standard trading size used by exchanges. Minimum lot size varies from exchange to exchange, and from one financial security to another.

low The lowest trade price during a specific trading period.

low latency Little or no delay; the term typically refers to the speed of order processing.

machine learning An adaptive computer program that updates its actions based on the most recent market information.

macroeconomic news News affecting the economy as a whole.

management fees Fees charged by mutual funds and hedge funds irrespective of the fund's performance.

margin The leverage provided in one's brokerage account.

margin call A request to add money to the brokerage account. The margin call is sent whenever one's brokerage account balance falls below a prespecified level, known as the maintenance margin. If the call is not satisfied in a timely manner, the brokerage liquidates securities held in the account.

mark-to-market A valuation of the financial securities in one's account at market prices.

market An aggregate of all trading activity. In its purest, most scientific sense, a market includes financial markets, real estate sales, and other liquid and illiquid transactions.

market efficiency A condition whereby the market prices reflect available news. The quicker the markets incorporate news, the more efficient are the markets.

market impact A temporary adverse movement of prices following a large sell or buy order. Market impact occurs due to a temporary shortage in supply or demand following execution of a large order.

market microstructure A close-up study of market movements, including the evolution of quotes, bid-ask spreads, and other minute market details.

market liquidity The same as *liquidity*.

market-neutral An investment strategy that seeks to neutralize broad market movements by buying some and selling other securities.

market order A trading order to be executed immediately at the best available price.

market participant A trader.

market regulation A set of laws governing market operations.

market risk A risk of loss resulting from market price movements of one's investment portfolio holdings.

Martingale A property of price evolution whereby the best estimate of the price in the next period of time is the current price level. Martingale securities are financial securities the prices of which obey the Martingale property.

maturity The end date of a financial contract; often used to specify the terms of futures, bonds, and other financial instruments. The maturity date is often followed by the "delivery date"—the date when either the principal is refunded or there is physical delivery of goods (say, bushels of corn in corn futures).

maximum-likelihood estimation (MLE) An econometric technique to find the most likely dependencies between various variables.

mean An average.

mean-reversion A property of selected variables where valuation over time migrates to the mean value. For example, prices of certain securities may have a tendency to revert to their mean levels.

mean-variance frontier A representation of relationships between means and variances of returns of various securities and portfolios of securities. The frontier comprises the securities and portfolios with the smallest variance for a given level of return.

model See *Statistical Model*

Monte-Carlo A statistical simulation of probable outcomes.

municipal bond A loan borrowed by a municipality from willing investors.

mutual fund A regulated investment fund that invests into buy-and-hold equity strategies.

neural network A feedback-based computer program that examines patterns of prices and other market variables and compares them with its previously recorded patterns. Neural networks can be used to identify complex market patterns.

nonlinear Not following a straight-line path.

nonparametric Nonparametrized.

open, high, low, close (OHLC) A sequence of prices typically reported for any chosen time period for any historical data other than tick data.

open price The first trade price within a specific trading period.

opportunity cost The implied cost when an investor allocates capital to other investment opportunities.

option-implied volatility The measure of volatility extracted from market option prices.

option A right, but not an obligation, to buy and sell securities.

option buyer A person or entity who buys an option.

option writer A person or entity who issues the option; option writers are obligated to honor their side of the option transaction.

order   A request to buy or sell a financial security.

order book   A log of a broker-dealer or an exchange that shows all open limit orders placed by clients at various prices.

order fill rate   A percentage of limit orders away from the market price that get executed.

order flow   Net size of buy orders less sell orders executed through an exchange or a broker-dealer during a specific time period.

order slicing   Separating a large trading order into a multitude of small trading orders.

out-of-sample   Results of a trading model back-test performed on data that was not used in the original model development. Out-of-sample back-test results are more objective than in-sample results.

out-of-the-money (OTM)   Nonprofitable at the moment; a term typically used with options.

over-the-counter (OTC)   Not traded on an exchange, but negotiated privately instead.

pairs trading   An investment strategy that identifies and bets upon pairs of securities in a long-short manner in order to minimize market exposure.

par   The notional value of the security. In bonds, the par is the principal amount.

parameter   A coefficient in a statistical model.

parametric   A relationship that can be statistically parametrized; a trading model that employs parameters.

parity   Priced on par with another financial security.

passive management   An investment style whereby an investor or a fund manager holds financial securities without frequent rebalancing.

performance fees   A percentage of return that is paid out to the fund management as an incentive to deliver high returns.

plot   A chart illustrating the relationship between two or three variables.

point forecast   The expected value.

portfolio   An aggregation of financial securities that one has chosen for investment. The term "portfolio" dates back to the time when ownership of any security was accompanied by a sheet of paper, a certificate. Investors then stored these certificates in leather portfolios. Today, ownership of most securities is recorded electronically only.

post-trade analysis   Analysis of the accuracy of an investment forecast, trade execution costs, speed, and other relevant factors.

predictability   The degree to which the movement of a variable can be forecast.

pre-trade analysis Estimation of trade risk and other factors relevant to the impending trade order.

price A market indicator of the fair value.

proprietary trading Trading for one's own account.

put An option to sell the underlying security at a prespecified price on or before the prespecified date.

quantitative Based on measurable data.

quote A price level at which one is willing to buy or sell a particular financial security at a given time.

r-squared A regression statistic indicating what percentage of variable movement is explained by the regression.

random Arbitrary, uncorrelated with any factors.

real dollars Value of a security adjusted for inflation.

real-time Current.

realized gain (loss) The gain (loss) recorded when an investment position is closed.

regression A statistical technique used to quantify the impact of one security on another.

retail Individual investors with net worth below $100,000.

return on investment Realized gain on investment expressed as a percentage of capital invested.

risk A measure of possible loss.

risk aversion A measure of how intolerant one is to risk. Risk aversion is specific to individual investors and fund managers.

risk-free rate The rate of return offered on securities that have little chance of defaulting, such as U.S. T-bills.

risk management A set of practices to minimize the investment risk.

sample size The number of observations used in estimation.

scenario analysis An estimation of various investment outcomes obtained by varying the underlying assumptions. Scenario analysis typically considers the base, best, and worst cases of realizations of macroeconomic variables, supply, demand, and so on.

secondary equity offering (SEO) Post-IPO issues of common shares.

Securities and Exchange Commission (SEC) The U.S. organization governing operations of equity exchanges, mutual funds, and other related organizations.

shareholder An owner of stock certificates of a corporation.

Sharpe ratio The average annual return less the annual risk-free rate, all divided by the annual volatility (the standard deviation of returns). The ratio is named after William Sharpe, a prominent scientist and winner of the Noberl Memorial Prize in Economics.

short To sell, the opposite of "to long"—to buy.

short-selling   Selling a financial security without having bought it first.

skewness   An indicator of whether the bulk of variables under consideration are positive or negative.

sovereign debt   Bonds issued by a government.

spot   Current.

spread   A difference between any two variables.

stationary   Possessing stationarity.

stationarity   A condition whereby the statistical properties of a variable remain stable through time.

statistical arbitrage   Trading on temporary deviations from stable statistical relationships.

statistical model   An equation or a set of equations describing behavior of one or more economic variables.

statistical significance   Indication of how stable is a particular statistical observation.

stock   A document giving its owner a vote of the stock-issuing corporation.

stock buy-back   The opposite of a stock issue.

stockholder   An owner of a stock.

stock market   An exchange or a trading venue, such as a dark pool.

stock split   An increase in the number of outstanding shares and the proportional break down in prices of stocks. Stock splits are typically conducted with the goal of keeping the stock prices within a specific range chosen by the issuing corporation.

stop loss   A trading order to limit risk on a losing security by closing the position.

strategy   An articulated trading procedure.

strategy capacity   The maximum amount of capital that is possible to infuse into an investment strategy without diluting the strategy performance.

structured product   A complex financial instrument.

swap   A financial contract in which one party agrees to swap its cash flows with those of another party. Swaps are commonly used in foreign exchange and interest rate hedging strategies.

synthetic security   A security constructed to mimic cash flows of another security. Synthetic securities are built and traded whenever the original security is unavailable or is temporarily mispriced.

systematic trading   Trading based on a clearly articulated process, known as the system.

t-ratio   A statistical measure indicating dispersion of a variable.

tail risk   The risk of extreme events.

theta   Sensitivity of a security price to time. Theta is commonly used in option pricing.

third-party research Research developed by an outside agency.

tick data Data comprising individual quotes and their time stamps.

time decay The erosion of value of a financial security close to the expiration of that security. The concept of time decay is often used in option investing.

time series A data set of a particular security property, ordered by time stamp.

time-weighted average price (TWAP) algorithm An algorithm that strives to achieve at least as good a trading price as the average price throughout a given trading period.

track record The historical performance of an investment, fund manager, or the like.

tracking error A discrepancy between returns of an original and synthetic security designed to mimic the former.

trading aggressiveness A degree to which an investor prefers using market orders versus limit orders.

trading volume The aggregate size of contracts traded during a specific period of time.

underlying A financial security on which a derivative instrument is based.

unrealized gain (loss) The market gain (loss) that would result if all open investment positions were instantaneously closed.

value-at-risk (VaR) An amount of capital subject to loss in the worst 5 or 1 percent of market conditions.

value investing An investing methodology that involves identifying undervalued financial securities relative to a pro forma valuation.

vanilla A simple financial instrument.

variable A quantifiable metric that changes over time.

variance Standard deviation squared.

vega Sensitivity of a financial derivative instrument to the volatility of the underlying asset.

volatility Price variation; most often expressed as a standard deviation of returns.

volume See *Trading Volume*.

volume-weighted average price (VWAP) An algorithm that strives to achieve at least as good a trading price as the average price realized over a certain trading volume.

voting rights The common-stock investor's right to elect directors of the corporation.

warrants Nontraded options.

year-to-date (YTD) From the beginning of the current year to now.

yield Same as the *internal rate of return*.

REFERENCES

Aldridge, Irene. 2009. *High-frequency trading: A practical guide to algorithmic strategies and trading systems.* Hoboken, NJ: John Wiley & Sons.

Aldridge, Irene and Steven Krawciw. 2010. "Portfolio concentration: A strategy in a downturn," Working Paper.

Badrinath, S.G., Jayant R. Kale, and Thomas H. Noe, 1995. "Of shepherds, sheep, and the cross-autocorrelations in equity returns." *Review of Financial Studies*: 401–430.

Barber, Brad, Terrance Odean, and Michal Strahilevets. 2004. "Once burned, twice shy: How naive learning and counterfactuals affect the repurchase of stocks previously sold." Working Paper.

Beaudry, Paul, and Franck Portier. 2006. "Stock prices, news, and economic fluctuations." *American Economic Review*: 1293–1307.

Bekaert, Geert, Robert J. Hodrick, and Xiaoyan Zhang. 2009. "International stock return comovements." *Journal of Finance*: 2591–2626.

Benjamin, John D., Peter Chinloy, and G. Donald Jud. 2004. "Real estate versus Financial wealth in consumption." *Journal of Real Estate Finance and Economics*: 341–354.

Bernanke, Ben S., and Vincent R. Reinhart. 2004. "Conducting monetary policy at very low short-term interest rates." *American Economic Review*: 85–90.

Bernard, Andrew B., J. Bradford Jensen, and Peter K. Schott. 2006. "Trade costs, firms and productivity." *Journal of Monetary Economics*: 917–937.

Blanchard, Olivier, Francesco Giavazzi, and Filipa Sa. 2005. "International investors, the U.S. current account, and the dollar." *Brookings Papers on Economic Activity.*

Blinder, Alan, and Louis Maccini. 1991. "Taking stock: A critical assessment of recent research on inventories." *Journal of Economic Perspectives*: 73–96.

Brennan, Michael J., Narasimhan Jegadeesh, and Bhaskaran Swaminathan. 1993. "Investment analysis and the adjustment of stock prices to common information." *Review of Financial Studies*: 799–824.

Choi, James J., David Laibson, Brigitte C. Madrian, and Andrew Metrick. 2009. "Reinforcement learning and savings behavior." *Journal of Finance*: 2515–2534.

Christiano, Lawrence, Cosmin Ilut, Roberto Motto, and Massimo Rostagno. 2008. "Monetary policy and stock market boom-bust cycles." European Central Bank, Working Paper Series 955.

Cohen, Lauren, and Breno Schmidt. 2009. "Attracting flows by attracting big clients." *Journal of Finance*: 2125–2151.

Cohen, Randolph B., Christopher Polk, and Tuomo Vuolteenaho. 2009. "The price is (almost) right." *Journal of Finance*: 2739–2782.

Cunningham, Thomas J. 2006. "The predictive power of the Senior Loan Officer Survey: Do lending officers know anything special?" Federal Reserve Bank of Atlanta, Working Paper 2006–24.

Desai, Mihir A. 2005. "The degradation of reported corporate profits." *Journal of Economic Perspectives*: 171–192.

Desai, Mihir A., and James R. Hines, Jr. 2007. "Market reactions to export subsidies." *Journal of International Economics*: 459–474.

Dreher, Axel, and Roland Vaubel. 2009. "Foreign exchange intervention and the political business cycle: A panel data analysis." *Journal of International Money and Finance*: 755–775.

Ehrmann, Michael, and Marcel Fratzscher. 2007. "Communication by Central Bank Committee members: Different strategies, same effectiveness?" *Journal of Money Credit and Banking*: 509–541.

Emmons, William R., Aeimit K. Lakdawala, and Christopher J. Neely. 2006. "What are the odds? Option-based forecasts of FOMC target changes." *Federal Reserve Bank of St. Louis Review*: 543–562.

Fang, Lily and Joel Peress. 2009. "Media coverage and the cross-section of stock returns." *Journal of Finance*: 2023–2052.

Freund, Caroline. 2005. "Current account adjustment in industrial countries." *Journal of International Money and Finance*: 1278–1298.

Gervais, Simon, Ron Kaniel, and Dan Mingelgrin. 2001. "The high-volume return premium." *Journal of Finance*: 877–919.

Gurkaynak, Refet, Brian Sack, and Eric Swanson. 2005. "Do actions speak louder than words? The response of asset prices to monetary policy actions and statements." *International Journal of Central Banking*: 55–93.

Heston, Steven L., and Ronnie Sadka. "Seasonality in the cross-section of stock returns: The international evidence." *Journal of Financial and Quantitative Analysis*, forthcoming.

Hong, Harrison, Walter Torous, and Rossen Valkanov. 2007. "Do industries lead stock markets?" *Journal of Financial Economics*: 367–396.

Irvine, Owen, and Scott Schuh. 2005. Sales persistence and the reductions in GDP volatility." Federal Reserve Bank of Boston, Working Paper No. 05-5.

Irvine, Owen, and Scott Schuh. 2007. "The roles of comovement and inventory investment in the reduction of output volatility." Federal Reserve Bank of Boston, Working Paper No. 05-9.

Jorion, Philippe and Gaiyan Zhang. 2009. "Credit contagion from counterparty risk." *Journal of Finance*: 2053–2087.

Kumar, Alok. 2009. "Who gambles in the stock market?" *Journal of Finance*: 1889–1933.

Linnainmaa, Juhani T. 2010. "Do limit orders alter inferences about investor performance and behavior?" *Journal of Finance*, forthcoming.

Lo, Andrew and Craig MacKinlay. 1990. "When are contrarian profits due to stock market overreaction?" *Review of Financial Studies*: 175–206.

Malmendier, Ulrike, and Stefan Nagel. 2007. "Depression babies: Do macroeconomic experiences affect risk-taking?" Working Paper.

Menzly, Lior and Oguzhan Ozbas. 2010. "Market segmentation and cross-predictability of returns." *Journal of Finance*: 1555–1580.

Næs, Randi, Johannes A. Skjeltorp, and Bernt Arne Ødegaard. 2010. "Stock market liquidity and the business cycle." Forthcoming, *Journal of Finance*.

Ni, Sophie Xiaoyan, Neil D. Pearson, and Allen M. Poteshman. 2005. "Stock price clustering on option expiration dates." *Journal of Financial Economics*: 49–87.

Savor, Pavel and Qi Lu. 2009. "Do stock mergers create value for acquirers?" *Journal of Finance*: 1061–1097.

Warnock, Francis E., and Veronica Cacdac Warnock. 2009. "International capital flows and U.S. interest rates." *Journal of International Money and Finance*: 903–919.

ABOUT THE AUTHORS

Irene Aldridge is a managing pa....r and quantitative portfolio manager at ABLE Alpha Trading, LTD. She is also a founder of AbleMarkets.com, an online resource bringing the latest quantitative securities research to institutional and retail investors.

Aldridge is the author of *High-Frequency Trading: A Practical Guide to Algorithmic Strategies and Trading Systems* (John Wiley & Sons, 2009). She regularly appears on business television, including CNBC, Fox Business, and *The Daily Show* with Jon Stewart, and has been quoted by the *Wall Street Journal*, Bloomberg, and Reuters. Aldridge is a frequent speaker at top industry events and a contributor to academic and practitioner publications, including the *Journal of Trading*, E-Forex, *HedgeWorld*, *FX Week*, FINalternatives, *Wealth Manager*, and Dealing With Technology.

Prior to ABLE Alpha, Aldridge worked for various institutions on Wall Street and in Toronto, including Goldman Sachs and CIBC. She taught finance at the University of Toronto. She holds an MBA from INSEAD, an MS in financial engineering from Columbia University, and a BE in electrical engineering from the Cooper Union in New York. In her spare time, Aldridge enjoys gardening, hosting parties for family and friends, and spending time at the beach, all the while seldom parting with her laptop.

Steven Krawciw is an executive at a top-tier global private bank. Over his career, Krawciw has managed private banking products and advised executives, heads of multinational companies, and government leaders while working for CIBC Wealth Management, McKinsey and Co., and Monitor Company. Among his most memorable past projects is facilitating infrastructure development of the then-nascent South African government of Nelson Mandela.

Steven has published in Wealth Manager and FINalternatives on hedge fund investing strategies for private investors.

Krawciw holds an MBA (Finance) from the Wharton School of the University of Pennsylvania and a B.Comm. with Distinction in economics from the University of Calgary. He is an avid runner, cyclist, and has scaled peaks on four continents. Krawciw lives in New York, NY.

INDEX

Note: Page numbers followed by "f" and "t" indicate figures and tables.

A

ABC News Consumer Comfort Index, 74–75
    example, 74f
Active management, 165
ADP Employment Report. *See* Automatic Data Processing, Inc.
Advanced GDP figures, 40
Affordability Index, housing measure, 90
Aggregate money base, increase, 134
Agricultural workers, 112
Algorithm, 165
Algorithmic trading, 165
All-equity portfolio, U.S. dollar denomination, 32
Alpha, 165
Alternative investment, 165
American option, 165
Analyst report, 165
Announcement, expectation, 6
Arbitrage, 165
ARCH. *See* Auto-Regressive Conditional Heteroskedasticity
Asset allocations, 165
   distortion, 36
Asymmetric information, 165–166
At-the-money (ATM), 166
Autocorrelation, 166

Automatic Data Processing, Inc. (ADP)
    employment report, 106t, 108–110
    changes, GBP/USD response, 110f
Auto-Regressive Conditional Heteroskedasticity (ARCH), 165
Average annual return, 166

B

Back-test, 166
Bank cash, 134
Banking stocks, trade, 132
Bank of England, MPC, 150
Bankruptcy, 166
Bank stocks
   recession, impact, 22–24
   reduction, 130–132
Barber, Brad, 38
Baskets, diversification, 28
Bayesian, 166
Beadry, Paul, 126
Bear market, 166
Bekaert, Geert, 24
Benjamin, John D., 134
Bernanke, Ben, 148
Bernard, Andrew, 127
Beta, 166
Bid-ask spreads, 9, 166
   latent execution cost, 13t

Black-Scholes equation, 166
Blanchard, Olivier, 94
Bondholder, 166
Bonds, 166
  portfolios, diversification, 32
  prices, driver, 100
Bottom-up approach, 4–5
Broker commissions, transparent execution
    cost, 13t
Broker-dealer, 166
Broker fees, accountability, 8–9
Bull market, 166
Bureau of Economic Analysis (BEA)
  corporate profits calculation/
      report, 48
  Current Account Balance, 94
  real GDP report, 40, 42
Bureau of Labor Statistics, EDI, 124
Bureau of the Census
  home vacancy index change report, 88
  monthly data, 58
Business Employment Dynamics, 106t
Buy-and-hold, 166
  strategies, 2, 9
Buy position (entry), limit order (usage), 11–12

C
Call, 167
Capacity, 167
Capacity utilization, 64–65
  report, insights, 65
Capital, 167
  flow. See International capital flow
  gain/loss, 167
  markets, 167
Capital Asset Pricing Model (CAPM), 167
Cash flow
  analysis, 36
  consistency, 20–22
CDSs. See Credit Default Swaps
Centralized trading volume, absence, 30
CFTC. See Commodity and Futures Trading
    Commission
Challenger, Gray & Christmas Employment
    Report, 114
Challenger Employment Report, 106t

Challenger Job-Cut Report, 114
  changes, S&P500 response, 114f
Chicago Federal Reserve Regional Survey, 56
Chinloy, Peter, 134
Choi, James, 38
Christiano, Lawrence, 127
Closing price, 167
Cloud computing, 167
Cohen, Lauren, 34, 36
Cohen, Randolph, 20
Cointegration, 167
Collateral, 167
Colocation, 167
Commercial banks, 140
Commodity, 167
Commodity and Futures Trading Commission
    (CFTC), 167
Comparable, 167
Competitive advantage framework, 122
Computer technology, complexity, 154
Conference Board, index of leading economic
    indicators, 58
Construction, 79
Construction spending
  changes, response, 82f
  data, 80
  impact, 80–82
Consumer comfort index. See ABC News
    Consumer Comfort Index
Consumer confidence, 67
  changes, company response (example), 72f
  impact, 72–73
Consumer credit report (U.S. Federal Reserve
    Board), 138–140
  changes, company response, 140f
Consumer goods, manufacturer new orders, 58
Consumer Price Index (CPI), 46, 116–118
  change. See U.S. Consumer Price Index
    change
  components, 116t
  computation, price data points, 116
Consumer profile (ABC), 74
Consumer purchases, impact, 68
Consumers, domestic spending, 42
Consumer sentiment. See U.S. Consumer
    Sentiment index

Consumer spending, 67
Contagion, 167
Convertible debt, 167
Corporate 401(k) plans, majority investor
  status, 34
Corporate activity (estimates), economic
  corporate profit figures (usage), 48
Corporate bond, 167
Corporate default, spread, 22
Corporate profits
  calculation methods, 48
  earnings basis. *See* Economic corporate
    profits
  economic indicator validity, 46–50
  measure, problem, 50
  quarterly tax filings, 48
  report, 46
Corporations
  financing gaps, 132
  401(k) asset placement (mutual fund
    manager rewards), 36
Correlation, 167
  measure, 28
  risk, impact, 28–30
Counterparty risk, 9, 10
Coupon, 167–168
Covariance, 168
CPI. *See* Consumer Price Index
Crash trading strategy, 28
Credit contagion, 22
Credit Default Swaps (CDSs), 154
Creditors, balance sheet (impact), 22
Credit rating, 168
Credit risk, 9, 10
Credit spread, 168
Credit unions, 140
Crude materials, PPI, 120
Cumulative returns, 162f
Cunningham, Thomas, 136, 138
Currencies
  circulation, 134
  short-term positions, 154
Currency pair, ETF tracking, 34
Current Account Balance (BEA), 92–94.
    See also U.S. Current Account
    Balance

quarterly changes, 92
  U.S. dollar, relationship, 94–96
Current Employment Statistics Survey`, 106t
  establishment survey, 112
Current Population Survey, 106t
  household survey, 112

D

Daily data, 168
Dark pools, 168
Data, accuracy, 108
Data mining, 5
Data points, 168
Data set, 168
Day order, 168
Debt/dividends, flows, 132
Default, 168
Default clustering, 22
Delivery, 168
Delta, 168
Demand, 168
Department of Commerce. *See* U.S.
    Department of Commerce
Department of Labor. *See* U.S. Department of
    Labor
Derivative, 169
Desai, Mihir, 124
Directional forecast, 168–169
Directional trade, 169
Distressed investing, 169
Diversification, 36. *See also* Baskets; Bond
    portfolios; International diversification
    success. *See* Stocks
Dividend, 169
Domestic economies, improvement, 122, 124
Domestic inflation, changes (forecast), 124
Domestic markets, portfolio exposure risk, 32
Domestic subsidies, 124
Drawdown, 169
Dreher, Axel, 136
Durable goods manufacturers, stocks (response), 62
Durable goods orders, 58–60
  changes, company response (example), 60f
  factory order percentage, 62
  U.S. Department of Commerce statistics, 60
Dynamic trading, 2

E

ECI. *See* Employment Cost Index

Econometrics, 169

Economic conditions, improvement, 60

Economic corporate profits

earnings basis, 48

figures, corporate activity estimate, 48

S&P500, contrast (example), 48f

Economic cycles, long-term bets (investor consideration), 94

Economic expansions/contractions (display), ISM index (usage), 54–56

Economic health (indication), PI (usage), 46

Economic indexes, 104

Economic indicator, corporate profits (usage), 46–50

Economic prosperity, free trade (stimulation), 122

Economic trends, Current Account Balance (usage), 92–94

Economy

forecast, flow of funds (usage), 132–134

private sector outlook, 42

stimulation, consumer purchases (impact), 68

Ehrmann, Michael, 150

Electronic trading, adoption, 154, 169

Emerging market, 169

Emmons, William, 152

Empire State Manufacturing Survey, 56

Employer-specific news, 36

Employment, 103, 110–113

economic indicator, 104

indexes, 106t

selection, 104

level/trending, 104

reporting, frequency, 104–108

statistics, 110

Employment Cost Index (ECI), 124–126

changes, 126

S&P500, relationship, 126f

Equities, 169

investment quality, 20–22

markets, homebuyer number decline (impact), 82–84

prices, reduction, 22

short-term position, 154

valuation, 22

Equity portfolios (hedging), foreign currencies (usage), 32–34

Error, 169

Establishment survey (Current Employment Statistics Survey), 112

ETFs. *See* Exchange-traded funds

Euro, U.S. dollar (contrast), 32

European Central Bank (ECB), Governing Council, 150

European option, 169

Event-based strategies, 8, 12

Event window, 169

Exchange fees, 169

accountability, 8–9

transparent execution cost, 13t

Exchange-traded funds (ETFs), 169

development, 28

list, 34t

purchase, 56

quant investing strategy, 27

sale, 28

short-term positions, 154

trading, correlation risk (impact), 28–30

Exchange-traded options, features, 158

Execution, 169

Execution costs

overview, 12

types/descriptions, 13t

Existing Home Sales, housing measure, 90

Existing single family homes, sale metric, 88

Expiration dates, 160, 169

Exponential, 169

Exporters, tax breaks, 124

Export prices. *See* Import/export prices

F

Factor model, 170

Factory orders

changes, company response (example), 62f

increases, 60

percentage, 62

Fang, Lily, 16

Farm income, 44

Federal balance sheet, changes (company response), 146f
Federal Budget Balance, 144–146
Federal Discount Window, 144
Federal Funds rate. *See* U.S. Federal Funds rate
nearest-expiration futures contracts, 152
Federal government finances, 141
Federal Open Market Committee. *See* U.S. Federal Open Market Committee
Federal Reserve. *See* U.S. Federal Reserve
Federal Reserve Bank, credit, 144
Finance companies, 140
Financial contract, 170
Financial data, 129
Financial institutions, borrowing/lending sources, 132
Financial instruments, cash transfer, 130
Financial securities
markets, capability, 108
trading, high-frequency returns, 2
Finished goods, PPI, 118
breakdown, 120t
Firms
cash flow consistency, 20–22
clientele, understanding, 22–24
credit relationship, examination, 22
stock price prediction, 20, 22
Firm-specific credit rating upgrades/downgrades, impact, 6
Firm-wide stability, employer-specific news, 36
Fixed-rate loans, losses, 132
Flight to quality, 16
Flow of funds, usage, 132–134
FOMC. *See* U.S. Federal Open Market Committee
Forecasting, 170
Foreign bonds, demand, 98
Foreign capital, net inflow, 96
Foreign currencies
purchase, 32, 34
U.S. dollar, weakening, 51
usage, 32–34
Foreign exchange, 170
centralized trading volume, absence, 30
investable asset, 30–32
investing, 98–100

markets, regulation (absence), 32
quant investing strategies, 27
rate, decline (observation), 5
values, decrease, 30, 32
Foreign trade, 91
Forward-looking indicators, 108
401(k) investments, 34–36
allocation method, 36–38
gains, 38
increase, 34, 36
mutual fund manager reward, 36
401(k) program, employee control (absence), 36
Fratzscher, Marcel, 150
Fraud (incidence), recession (impact), 62
Freund, Caroline, 92
Fundamental analysis, 170
Fundamentals-based concentration strategy, 28
Fund-of-funds, 170
Fund replication, 170
Funds, net unilateral transfers, 94, 96
Future cash flows, present value calculation, 20
Futures, 170–171
short-term positions, 154
Future technological opportunities, news, 126

G
GARCH. *See* Generalized ARCH
GDP. *See* Gross Domestic Product
Generalized ARCH (GARCH), 165
Gervais, Simon, 16
Giavazzi, Francesco, 94
Global Tactical Asset Allocation (GTAA), 171
Goods/services
Current Account Balance, 94, 96
imports/exports, report (release), 96
net exports, 50–51
trade, 94
Good-Till-Cancel (GTC) order, 171
Good-till-cancel limit order, investor setting, 11
Government Consumption Expenditures, 42
GPDI. *See* Gross Private Domestic Investment
Gross Domestic Product (GDP). *See* Real GDP Seasonally Adjusted Annual Rate
components, growth (example), 44f

Gross Domestic Product (GDP) *(cont.)*
  figures
    abstraction, 40, 42
    example, 40f
  future growth, forecast, 136
  growth, senior loan officer insight, 136–138
  movements, 138, 138t
  questions, 138t
  reporting stages, 40
  reports, impact, 40–42
Gross Investments, 42
Gross Private Domestic Investment (GPDI),
    stock market (relationship), 42–44
GTAA. *See* Global Tactical Asset Allocation
GTC. *See* Good-Till-Cancel
Gurkaynak, Refet, 126

H
Hedge funds, 171
  long-short investing, 2
Hedging, 171
  securities involvement, 9–10
Help Wanted Advertising Index, 106t
Heston, Steven L., 160, 162
Heteroscedasticity, 171
High-frequency trading (HFT), 154–156, 171
High net worth, 171
High price, 171
High watermark, 171
Hines, James, 124
Histogram, 171
Historical data, 171
Hodrick, Robert, 24
Holding horizon, expiration, 9
Holding period, 171
Homebuyers, number (decline), 82–84
Homeowner occupancy rates, 88
  assessment, 90
Home vacancy indexes, changes (Bureau of the
    Census), 88
Households, national survey, 72
Household survey (Current Population
    Survey), 112
Housing, 79
  sector, stability (index), 86
Housing data, precision (requirement), 88–90

Housing Market Index (HMI), NAHB prepara-
    tion, 88
Housing Starts and Building Permits, 88
Housing Vacancies and Homeownership
    Rates, 88

I
Iceberg order, 171
ICSC Retail Sales Index, 74
Ilut, Cosmin, 127
Import/export prices, 120–124
Import prices, changes, 124
Income. *See* National income; Personal income
Income,
Indebtedness, relative level, 132
Index, 171
Index of leading economic indicators
    (Conference Board), 58
Industrial firms, bank credit extension, 22
Industrial production, 64–65
  changes, EUR/USD response, 64f
  increase, 65
Inflation, 171
  increase, 134
Initial Public Offering (IPO), 171–172
In-sample, 172
Institute for Supply Management (ISM)
  index, 54–56
  Manufacturing Index
    market reaction, 54, 56
    S&P5000 response, 54f
  monthly reports, 56
Institutional, term (usage), 172
Institutional investors, stock avoidance, 18
Interest rates, 148–151, 172
  announcements, 150
  decisions (U.S. FOMC), 150
  decline. *See* U.S. interest rates
  distilling, 152
  forecasts, 152
  maintenance, 148
Intermediate goods/supplies/components,
    PPI, 120
Internal rate of return, 172
International capital flow, 91
International diversification, 24–26

International stock markets, observed
  correlation (absence), 24
International trade
  balance (changes), S&P500 (response), 96f
  costs, decrease, 127
  figures, 98
  increase, 96–98
  trends, 94
Interventionism, defense, 122, 124
In-the-money (ITM), term (usage), 172
In the money options, 152
Intra-month volatility, pattern (recurrence),
  160
Inventories, 53, 172
Investable assets, 30–32
Investing, 172
  style, 172
Investment
  banking, 172
  decision-making, intuition (usage), 3
  delay, latent execution cost, 13t
  funds, U.S. households (assets distribution), 132
  horizons, usage, 22
  positions, investor monitoring, 11
  process, 8–9
  risk, reduction, 28
Investment strategies, production, 5
Investors
  goals/risk profiles, 38
  income level, 38
  positions, active monitoring, 11
IPO. *See* Initial Public Offering
iShares Dow Jones U.S. Home Construction ETF
  changes, 72
  response, 76
ISM. *See* Institute for Supply Management
Issuer, 172
ITM. *See* In-the-money

J
Japanese yen (FXY), examination, 34
Jensen, Bradford, 127
Job Opening and Labor Turnover Survey
  (JOLTS), 106t
Johnson Redbook Report, 70–71
  changes, EUR/USD response, 70f

Jorion, Philippe, 22
Jud, G. Donald, 134

K
Kaniel, Ron, 16
Kansas City Federal Reserve Bank
  Manufacturing Survey, 56
Kumar, Alok, 18
Kurtosis, 172

L
Labor compensation, 44
Lakdawala, Aeimit, 152
Latent execution costs, 13t
Leader-follower phenomena, 158t
Legal risk, 9, 10
Leverage, 172
Limit order, 11–12, 172
  attractiveness, 11
  investor placement, 11
Linear, term (usage), 172
Linnainmaa, Juhani T., 11
Liquidity, 7, 172
  change, 16
  drivers, 16
  pool, 172
  problems, 144
  risk, 9, 10, 172
  usage, 16–17
Long, term (usage), 172
Longer-term Fed credits, extension, 144
Long position (entry), limit order
  (usage), 12
Long-short, 173
Long-short quantitative investing, 2
Long-term investments, 92–94
Long-term stock returns, reduction, 16
Long-term U.S./foreign securities, purchases/
  sales balance (report), 98
Lot size, 172
Lottery tickets
  jackpot value, 18
  stocks, comparison, 18
Low, term (usage), 173
Low-dispersion forecasts, 152
Lu, Qi, 20

M

M1 variables, 130
M3 variables, 130
Machine learning, 173
Macroeconomic announcements, knowledge/
  news, 5–6, 36
Macroeconomic news, 173
Majority investor status, 34
Management fees, 173
Manpower Employment Outlook Survey, 106t
Manufacturers, shipments/inventories/orders,
  60–63
Manufacturing
  components, 64
  firms output/utilization, Federal Reserve
    report, 64
Manufacturing Index, ISM report, 54
Margin, 173
  call, 173
Market, 173
  impact, 173
  liquidity, 173
  microstructure, 173
  order, 173
  participant, 173
  regulation, 173
  risk, 173
Market bond yield, Fed consideration, 102
Market crashes
  mutual funds/ETFs, sale, 28
  stocks, purchase, 28
Market efficiency, 173
Market-neutral, 173
Market prices
  level, reduction, 12
  movement, 11
  phenomena, impact, 5–6
Market risk, 9–10
  expression, 9
Markets
  consumer confidence, impact, 72–73
  data, 152
  GDP reports, impact, 40–42
  impact, latent execution cost, 13t
  liquidity, measure, 16
  orders, profitability (reduction), 11

participants, collective beliefs/information,
  122
productivity news, impact, 126–127
volatility, 44
Markets, monitoring (investor ability), 11
Mark-to-market, 173
Martingale, 174
Maturity, 174
Maximum-Likelihood Estimation (MLE), 174
MBA purchase applications, changes (S&P500
  response), 8of
Mean, 174
Mean-reversion, 174
Mean-variance frontier, 174
Medium-term lock-ups, 130
Mines, Federal Reserve report, 64
Mingelgrin, Dan, 16
MLE. See Maximum-Likelihood Estimation
Monday effect, 162–164
  cause, 164
  trading patterns, impact, 164
Monetary Aggregates (U.S. Federal Reserve),
  130
Monetary base
  expansions. See Stealth monetary base
    expansions
  measures, 134
Monetary Committee (U.S. Federal Reserve),
  100
Monetary data, 129
Monetary Policy Committee (MPC), Bank of
  England, 150
Money loss, risk, 132
Money supply
  announcements, banking stocks (trade), 132
  increase, 132
Monster Employment Index, 106t
Monte Carlo (simulation), 174
Mortgage applications, index, 84
Mortgage Bankers Association (MBA)
  homebuyer index, 82
  indices, 84
Mortgage Delinquencies and Foreclosures, 88
Motto, Roberto, 127
MPC. See Monetary Policy Committee
Municipal bond, 174

Mutual funds, 174
    assets, amount, 34
    development. *See* Passive mutual funds
    expected returns, 36
    investments, 401(k) proportion, 34
    long-only investing, 2
    quant investing strategies, 27
    sale, 28

N
Næs, Randi, 16
National Association of Home Builders
        (NAHB), HMI preparation, 88
National Association of Realtors, indices, 90
National income, 39
National output, 39
Nearest-expiration futures contracts, 152
Neely, Christopher, 152
Net exports, 50–51
Net unilateral transfers, 94
Net Unilateral Transfers of Funds, 96
Neural network, 174
New home sales, changes (company response),
        84f
New single family home sales, impact, 84
Ni, Sophie Xiaoyan, 160
Nondefense capital goods, manufacturer new
        orders, 58
Nondurable goods orders, U.S. Department of
        Commerce statistics, 60
Non-farm individual proprietors' income, 44
Nonfinancial business, 140
Nonlinear, term (usage), 174
Nonparametric, term (usage), 174
Nonrevolving credit, 140

O
Observed phenomena, impact, 5–6
Odean, Terrance, 38
Ødegaard, Bernt Arne, 16
OFHEO Home Price Index, 90
OHLC. *See* Open, High, Low, Close
Open, High, Low, Close (OHLC), 174
Open market operations, 146
Open markets, Fed bonds (impact), 100, 102
Open price, 174

Operational malfunctions, losses (risk), 10
Operational risk, 9, 10
Opportunity costs, 174
    accountability, 9
    latent execution cost, 13t
Option-implied volatility, 174
Options, 174
    buyer, 174
    contracts, 156
    expiration
        data, effect, 160
        price discontinuity, 160
        trading, 156–160
    short-term positions, 154
    strike price, 156
    usage, 152
    writer, 174
Order book, 175
Order fill rate, 175
Order flow, 175
Orders, 53, 175
    execution, investor urgency, 11
Orders, selection, 11–12
Order slicing, 175
OTC. *See* Over-the-counter
OTM. *See* Out-of-the-money
Outlook surveys, 108
Out-of-sample, 175
Out-of-the-money (OTM), 175
Outstanding consumer credit, issuers
        (classifications), 140
Over-the-counter (OTC), 175
Over-the-counter (OTC) options, 156

P
Pairs trading, 175
Par, 175
Parameter, 175
Parametric, term (usage), 175
Parity, 175
Passive management, 175
Passive mutual funds, development, 28
Past performance, reliance (statistical
        rationale), 38
Pattern recognition, 5
PCE. *See* Personal consumer expenditures

Pearson, Neil D., 160
Pending Home Sales, housing measure, 90
Peress, Joel, 16
Performance fees, 175
Personal consumer expenditures (PCE)
 breakdown, 46t
 index, 46
Personal Consumption Expenditure, growth,
 42
Personal Income (PI), 44–46
 figures, reporting (timing), 44
Per-trade analysis, 176
Phenomenon (phenomena), impact, 5–6
Philadelphia Federal Reserve Business Outlook
 Survey, 56
 changes, security prices (correlations), 58t
Philadelphia Federal Reserve Index, U.S. secu-
 rities prices correlation, 56–58
PI. *See* Personal Income
Plot, 175
Point forecast, 152, 175
Polk, Christopher, 20
Portfolio, 175
 domestic market exposure risk, 32
 return, enhancement, 30
Portier, Franck, 126
Post-trade analysis, 175
Poteshman, Allen M., 160
PPI. *See* Producer Price Index
Predictability, 175
Pre-election spending, 136
Preliminary GDP figures, 40
Price, 176
 indexes, 120, 122
 relative changes, measure, 120, 122
Prices, 115
 appreciation, latent execution cost, 13t
 behavior, example, 30
 changes (measurement), PCE index (usage),
  46
 run-ups, impact, 5–6
Private firms, risk reduction, 42
Private household workers, 112
Private-sector nonfarm payrolls, ADP
  Employment Report measurement, 110
Producer Price Index (PPI), 118–120

changes. *See* U.S. Producer Price Index
 changes
Productivity, 115
 news, impact, 126–127
 realized gains, 126–127
Professional investors, stock avoidance,
 18
Proprietary trading, 176
Publicity, impact, 16
Purchase-specific lending, 140
Put, 176

Q
Quality, flight, 16
Quant Investor Almanac
 mathematical constructs, avoidance, 7–8
 usage
  advantage, maximization, 14
  process, 12, 14
Quantitative, term (usage), 176
Quantitative easing, 148
Quantitative investing (quantitative
  investment)
 costs, 12
 definition, 1–2
 figures, usefulness, 108
 long-only/long-short characteristics, 1–2
 process, 8–9
  explanation, 2–3
 traditional investing, contrast, 3
Quantitative investing (quantitative investment)
  strategies, 27, 156
 capacity, change, 7
 discovery, 4–5
 duration, 8
 ideas, 15
 investment level, 7
 mathematical underpinning, 4
 reasons, 4
Quantitative investors, orders (selection), 11–12
Quantitative strategy, development, 3–4
Quantitative traders (quants)
 practitioners, 1
 strategies, running, 6–7
Quote, 176
 information, 154

R
Random, term (usage), 176
Real dollars, 176
Real estate wealth, dollar (spending), 134
Real GDP, BEA report, 40, 42
Real GDP Seasonally Adjusted Annual Rate
    (SAAR) figures, 42
Realized gain/loss, 176
Real-time, term (usage), 176
Recession
    impact, 22–24, 62
    recovery, 65
Redbook. *See* Johnson Redbook Report
Refinancing applications, 84
Regional Federal Reserve surveys, 56–58
Regression, 176
Reinhart, Vincent R., 148
Rental income, 44
Reported payrolls, rise/fall, 110
Reporting, frequency, 104–108
Reserve Bank Credit, increase, 144
Residential delinquencies/foreclosures,
    quarterly index, 88
Residential mortgage applications, 84
Residential real estate
    household investments, 132
    market, value, 86
Retail, 176
Retailers, aggregate sales (U.S. Department of
    Commerce), 68
Retail sales
    changes, company response (example), 68f
    index, short-term impact, 68–70
Return on investment (ROI), 176
Revised GDP figures, 40
Richmond Federal Reserve Survey, 56
Richmond Federal Reserve Survey of Business
    Activity, 56
Risk, 176
    adjustment, 18
    amounts, 146
    aversion, 176
    management, 9–10, 176
    minimization, 30
    reduction, 24
Risk-free rate, 176

ROI. *See* Return on investment
Rostagno, Massimo, 127
R-squared, 176

S
Sa, Filipa, 94
SAAR. *See* Real GDP Seasonally Adjusted
    Annual Rate
Sack, Brian, 126
Sadka, Ronie, 160, 162
Sample size, 176
Savings rate, 132
Savor, Pavel, 20
Scenario analysis, 176
Schmidt, Breno, 34, 36
Schott, Peter, 127
Seasonality, trading, 162
Secondary Equity Offering (SEO), 176
Sectoral production/orders/inventories, 53
Securities
    average volume (liquidity), 7
    expected returns, 36
    generational preferences, 38
    markets, historic reaction, 104
    optimal price level, 8–9
    risk/return characteristics, 9–10
    target price, determination, 8–9
    types, 142
Securities, shorting, 2
Securities and Exchange Commission (SEC),
    176
Securities price
    determination, 8–9
        quantitative strategy, usage, 2–3
    level, 3
    past responses (description), event-based
        strategies (usage), 8
    Philadelphia Federal Reserve Business
        Outlook, changes (correlation), 58t
Securitized assets, pools, 140
Security-specific strategies, 8
Self-employed, 112
Self-regulating mechanisms, 122
Senior loan officer, poll, 136
SEO. *See* Secondary Equity Offering
Shareholder, 176

Sharpe ratio, 176
Shocks, price adjustment, 122
Short, term (usage), 177
Short-selling, 177
Short-term consumer credit, 138
Short-term deposits, 130
Short-term market volatility, investor control, 12
Single family home sales, impact, 84–86
Skewness, 177
Skjeltorp, Johannes A., 16
Social Security, 44
Spot, term (usage), 177
Spread, 177
Standard & Poor's 500 (S&P500)
  decline, 32, 82, 98
  ECI, relationship, 126f
  economic corporate profits, contrast (example), 48t
Standard & Poor's/Case-Shiller Home Price Index, 86–88
  example, 86f
State insurance-fraud bureaus, survey, 62
Stationarity, 177
Stationary, term (usage), 177
Statistical arbitrage, 177
Statistical correlations, impact, 5–6
Statistical significance, 177
Stealth monetary base expansions, 134–136
Stock-for-firm acquisition, completion, 20
Stockholder, 177
Stock markets, 177
  changes, ECI lag, 124, 126
  global integration level, 24
  gross private domestic investments, relationship, 42–44
  publicity, negative impact, 16
Stocks, 177
  buy-back, 177
  correlations
    display, 28
    trends, detection, 24–26
  diversification, success, 30
  examination, 18
  fair price, 20
  follower, 156
  fundamental values, purchase, 28

leader, 156
lottery ticket, investor treatment, 18
momentum, 156
overvaluation, 20
price, predictor, 20, 22
purchase, 56
quant investing strategy, 15
returns
  correlation, 28
  predictability, 16–17
  rise, 160–162
  split, 177
  trading volume, usage, 16–17
Stop loss, 177
Stop-loss order, placement, 10
Strahilevets, Michal, 38
Strategy, 177
  capacity, 177
Strike prices, 152, 156
Structured product, 177
Supply shocks, impact, 24
Swanson, Eric, 126
Swap, 177
Synthetic security, 177
Systematic trading, 177

T
Tail risk, 177
Target price, 8
Taxes, transparent execution costs, 13t
Taylor Nelson Sofres survey, 72
Technical analysis, 20
Term deposits, 130
Texas Manufacturing Outlook Survey, 56
Theta, 177
Third-party research, 178
Tick data, 154, 178
TICS. *See* Treasury International Capital System
Time decay, 178
Time series, 178
Time-Weighted Average Price (TWAP) algorithm, 178
Timing risk, latent execution cost, 13t
TIPS. *See* Treasury Inflation Protected Securities
Top-down approach, 4–5